Voices Everywhere

The Mysterious
Doris Stokes Effect

Linda Dearsley

DARK
RIVER

Published in 2019 by Dark River, an imprint of Bennion Kearny Limited.

Copyright © Dark River 2019

ISBN: 978-1-911121-53-4

Linda Dearsley has asserted her right under the Copyright, Designs and Patents Act, 1988 to be identified as the author of this book.

Published by Dark River, Bennion Kearny Limited
6 Woodside
Churnet View Road
Oakamoor
ST10 3AE

www.BennionKearny.com

To the one and only Doris Stokes.

With love and thanks.

INTRODUCTION

'There are more things in heaven and earth...' said Hamlet. So, was Shakespeare onto something all those years ago?

Driving past an unassuming village pub near the M1, not long ago, I was surprised to see a large board on the pavement outside on which someone had chalked – in big, rainbow letters – 'PSYCHIC NITE. 7.30.'

How odd, I thought. The streets were deserted, the village small, and it was starting to rain. Where would they find enough interested customers all the way out here? Yet, the following week, the board was out again, the words 'PSYCHIC NITE' now embellished with extravagant pink and blue chalk swirls. So, presumably, enough of an audience had materialised from somewhere to make the 'nite' worth repeating.

A few weeks later, passing through a town some distance away on a Sunday morning, I noticed purple balloons bobbing around the entrance of a community hall, and a queue of people stretching all the way up the road. A large banner over the door announced: 'Psychic Craft Fayre'. Clearly, a treat tempting enough to lure large numbers out of bed, early on a weekend.

And as I travelled around the country over the next months, I saw similar home-made notices sprouting up all over the place. There were invitations to Psychic Suppers, Psychic Events, Evenings of Clairvoyance, plus Mind, Body and Spirit Festivals. These were clearly not slick, professionally-organised, corporate affairs; in fact, some looked distinctly amateurish. They appeared to be spontaneous, local events put on by the people, for the people. And up and down the country, the people were coming, in their hundreds if not thousands.

On TV too, shows such as Most Haunted, Ghost Story, and Paranormal Adventures seemed to be multiplying daily, presumably because they were finding an eager fan base.

And all this, despite the fact that in the media the accepted view seems to be that the supernatural is (obviously) at best a joke, at worst a primitive superstition. All right-thinking people know that psychics are shameless frauds, don't they? They know that so-called 'psychic abilities' are underpinned by nothing more than cheap trickery, easily explained away by logic – because, how could they possibly be anything else?

Yet, strangely, no amount of intellectual scorn, disapproval, and – occasionally – insult appears to dent the stubborn enthusiasm for all things psychic. The rag-tag army of self-proclaimed mediums, psychics, healers, tarot-card readers, shamans, and angel oracles just seem to shrug its shoulders and keep on growing. What's more, peek inside the psychic events, and the majority of 'readers' offering their esoteric services would appear to be normal people, unknown to the police, who seem to conduct the other aspects of their lives honestly. Many claim that during the week they pursue ordinary, down-to-earth careers – they're builders, teachers, hairdressers, nurses, and so on – while others seem to be retired grandmas with lifelong records of good behaviour, unblemished by so much as a parking ticket.

Can all these inoffensive-looking characters really be ruthless con-artists beneath their smiles? If so, what would make so many ordinarily law-abiding people take up a little light fraud and deception in their spare time?

Or, could it be that just a percentage of them are con-artists and the rest, sincere but hopelessly deluded? At these events, are we witnessing a mass outbreak of cold-hearted, criminality? Or an epidemic of peculiar mental breakdown? Because, according to the logic of 'right-thinking people', these 'so-called psychics' must be either slightly mad, or slightly bad. There's nothing really in-between.

And what of the people who flock to consult them? Many of whom seem quite satisfied with the results they receive. So satisfied, in fact, they willingly return. Are they simply gullible or desperate? Too dull to realise they're being manipulated? Or too attention-starved to care?

These believers are a real puzzle to the cynics. Most of them seem well aware that the world is full of scoffers, yet still they persist in beliefs that the critics insist are irrational.

Is this what GK Chesterton meant when he said, 'When people stop believing in God, they don't believe in nothing, they believe in anything'?

Or to quote another great man (Dr. Johnson), yet another example of: 'The triumph of hope over experience'.

Yet, perhaps, it's always been this way. The belief in ghosts, witches, fortune-tellers, and strange, non-human creatures that lurk in the dark has clung on down the centuries. Shakespeare appreciated the dramatic possibilities of these ideas 500 years ago, and we're still lapping them up them today. We call it superstition. And you'd think superstition would have evaporated in the harsh glare of our digital, scientific 21st century. Yet, in recent years, we've even added another layer. Now we have aliens and flying saucers to add to the brew.

So what's going on? People are voting with their feet. Substantial numbers – seemingly neither mad nor bad – 'just know'. They instinctively feel that Shakespeare was right the first time. There is more in heaven and earth. What's more, they reckon they've found it.

And as I passed that 'Psychic Nite' blackboard yet again (yes, it seems to be a regular event. I really must look in some time), it occurred to me that I've known quite a number of these unusual people over the years. I've seen them up close, and I've seen them in action, so perhaps my experiences might shed some light on the puzzle.

It all began with an unassuming pensioner, introduced to me as Mrs Fisher Stokes, who said she heard voices. Doris Stokes, as she went on to become known to the world a few years later, truly caused a sensation. She attracted adulation and also savage criticism along the way. The sceptics said she was a dishonest fake, and that her fans were clearly deluded and gullible.

Yet plenty of perceptive, educated people took her seriously; people including the then-Bishop of Southwark, Mervyn Stockwood (who invited her to give him a reading in Southwark Palace), five-star US General Omar Bradley (who came to her London flat on a visit to the UK), and the young woman who was to go on to become the first woman Prime Minister of Pakistan, Benazir Bhutto.

So what are we to make of this conundrum? Who is right and who is wrong? And if there is more in Heaven and Earth than we ever dreamed possible – what exactly can it be? Read on and make up your own mind...

CHAPTER 1

It was one of those long, hot summers of the seventies. London was awash with flared jeans, platform soles, and strappy tops. Out in the streets, the tarmac was melting, talk of a bizarre, barely-believable new anti-music, anti-fashion craze called punk – involving a lot of safety-pins and spitting apparently – were beginning to circulate, but most people just laughed and longed for cool breezes, the seaside, and endless ice-cream.

Which made it the perfect moment – the Features Editor decided one morning, chewing her pen thoughtfully as the sun sweltered in through the non-opening windows of our new office – for a light, not too serious series on the supernatural.

Our woman's magazine had only recently moved into brand new offices on the South Bank at the time. A move that hadn't gone down too well with the staff. It wasn't just that to the untrained eye, our new home was a 30-storey, gun-metal tower of extreme ugliness with windows that didn't open, air-conditioning that didn't work properly, and lifts that broke down so regularly many preferred to take their chances in the dark shadows of the 'axe murderer' staircases.

No, it was the location that upset everyone. Back then, the South Bank wasn't the stylish, buzzy place it is today. Down-river from the Festival Hall and the National Theatre where we found ourselves plonked, weeds sprouted from derelict sites, there were pot-holed streets, boarded-up buildings, abandoned warehouses, and old-fashioned tramps with string around their waists and multiple carrier bags in their fists. They often staggered along shouting angry but incomprehensible insults.

Up the road, Cardboard City – named for the hundreds of rough sleepers who congregated there on beds made from cardboard boxes – was already beginning to form in the gloomy warren of underpasses that led to Waterloo station.

Around our tower, there was not a shop, restaurant or sandwich bar to be seen.

Quite a culture shock for the mainly young, mainly female employees so abruptly torn from the magazine's previous HQ in genteel Covent Garden. In fact, the area seemed such a depressing desert, the management laid on a staff canteen plus lunch-time coach to ferry us back and forth across the river to civilisation.

And so, that particular summer morning, having survived the gauntlet of Cardboard City and the dash up the concrete axe-murderer stairs, I arrived in our glass partitioned writers' pen to find my work from the day before more or less complete, making me, by pure chance, the only one of the magazine's three young reporters free to take on a new project. Which is how I ended up being assigned to the Features Editor's three-part series on the supernatural – for no other reason than that I happened to be available.

There was nothing to suggest this story would be any different from the hundreds I tackled in my time at the magazine. Our work was just 'tomorrow's fish and chip wrappers' after all, as the old hands frequently reminded us cub-reporters if we showed signs of getting above ourselves. I would have been astounded if I'd known this story was to have a lasting significance on me; a story that would continue to reverberate down the years.

At the time, of course, my only concern was where to start? There was no internet to help with research in those days; no Google, in fact no computers either. We worked with typewriters, paper, the company newspaper cuttings library and the phone (landline only, of course). Mobiles were a futuristic fantasy few of us even dreamed about. If we needed to make a call out of doors, we had to hunt the streets for a good old red telephone box.

What we did have, though, was an efficient and completely free, Directory Enquiry Service as well as public libraries in every town equipped with a full set of telephone directories. They covered the whole country and listed names and full addresses, as well a phone numbers. An incredibly valuable resource for journalists.

'Give Psychic News a call,' suggested the Features Editor. This, as the name suggested, was a newspaper devoted entirely to psychic and spiritual stories, and I could find the number through Directory Enquiries. 'Ask them if there's anyone they can recommend to talk to. We can make part one of the series an interview with a psychic.'

So I rang Psychic News.

'Well,' said Tony Ortzen, the helpful young reporter who picked up the phone, 'there's this medium just down from Lancashire we're hearing good reports about. Haven't met her yet, but her name's Doris Fisher Stokes and she lives in London now. Convenient for you from your office. Try her. And if that doesn't work for you, come back to me, and I'll think of someone else.'

So I rang the number he gave me.

Almost immediately a friendly, Lincolnshire voice answered. (It turned out that though Doris had been living in Lancaster; she was born and brought up in Grantham and never quite lost the accent.) And this, of course, was Doris herself. 'Yes, that'll be alright love,' she said cheerfully when I explained about needing someone to interview for the feature, 'When would you like to come?'

We were always advised to say 'as soon as possible' in reply to this question, so 'As soon as possible,' I replied. I expected Doris to offer 'the day after tomorrow' if I was lucky, or 'a week Wednesday' if I wasn't.

But Doris wasn't your usual kind of interviewee.

'Let's see,' she said, 'It's twelve now, and I've got the hairdressers at half past, and then I've got a bit of shopping to do, but I'll be back by two. Come at two?'

I had been expecting a fairly relaxed day, but that made me sit up.

'Great!' I said, surprised to be taken so literally. No time to laze around. I hadn't even had a chance to give the story any thought. What did I actually want to know from Doris? I'd have to think of some questions, fast. And find the A-Z map – the other essential piece of a reporter's kit. In those days, we navigated our way around London peering at the tiny black and white streets in our dog-eared editions of the famous paperback atlas.

*

Doris turned out to live on the other side of town, behind Fulham Broadway Station in a big complex built just after World War I for disabled ex-servicemen.

Originally intended for veterans returning from the front after World War 1, the Fisher Stokes (Doris and husband John) qualified for a flat here, I discovered later, because John was an ex-paratrooper who'd been badly wounded at Arnhem in World War II. Months after being informed her husband was 'missing, presumed dead' following the battle, Doris eventually discovered John had, in fact, been injured and was a prisoner of war. When hostilities ended, John finally returned home with a metal plate in his head and mild brain damage. He was never quite the same man again, but the couple remained completely devoted to each other.

Today the flats – backing onto Chelsea Football ground – are smart and desirable; modernised out of all recognition. But, back then, behind the imposing exterior, Sir Oswald Stoll Mansions offered pretty basic accommodation. The flats were arranged in dour, red-brick buildings with austere walkways and concrete staircases, overlooking a communal yard. Doris and John's second floor home had an indoor W.C. but no bathroom. If they fancied a soak, they used the tin bath that hung on the back of the kitchen door. And the front door opened into a tiny hall complete with big cupboard in which to store the coal.

Not that this fazed Doris. Though she jokingly referred to the place as 'Sing Sing' after the notorious New York jail, she and John seemed very happy with their London life. She'd even decorated the walkway outside their front door with pots of geraniums. A couple of folded deck-chairs were propped up against the wall. Presumably, whenever some warm sunshine penetrated the narrow aperture between the walkway wall and the floor above, the Fisher Stokes liked to sit outside their front door, catching the rays (for all the world as if they were on the beach in Blackpool).

The two of them were walking across the yard, criss-crossed with washing lines and flapping laundry when I arrived. John was carrying a bag of groceries, and Doris was searching through her purse for her key.

In later life, Doris became quite frail, but back then she was a tall, strong-looking woman – taller than her husband – with a halo of thick, springy grey hair that she was forever trying to subdue.

'Hello luv,' she said, 'Come on up.'

She had a warm smile and strikingly blue eyes. I don't know what I expected – knowing nothing about real life psychics – but from the films I'd seen, a flowing kaftan, hoop earrings and a distracted, other-worldly air seemed essential.

Doris, on the other hand, looked bafflingly normal as she strode up the stairs. When we got indoors, the first thing she did was light up a decidedly non-spooky cigarette.

So there we were in the snug sitting room, with its leatherette armchairs grouped around the old fashioned TV on which Doris loved to watch Coronation Street; there was an electric fire in the hearth and ginger cat dozing on the window sill. 'That's Matey,' said Doris.

John brought cups of tea and then tactfully withdrew. Doris lit up another cigarette as the phone rang, which it repeatedly did, with a client wanting to book an appointment.

'I charge £5 a sitting,' she explained when she finished the call, 'which may sound a lot (equivalent to around £20 today) but I only do two sittings a day, one in the morning and one in the afternoon. Some people think it's easy, just sitting on your bottom all day, but even if it doesn't look like it, it's hard work.'

Even then she was puzzled and a little hurt that some people felt it was wrong to make a charge. 'I mean even vicars get paid, don't they?' she said. 'Everyone's got to live.'

Yet, she clearly enjoyed her work. 'When you see someone walk in here, miserable and grieving,' said Doris sipping her tea, 'and then walk out an hour later smiling, it makes you feel so good.'

She was a great talker, that's for sure. I scribbled away, filling page after page of my notebook, wishing I'd paid more attention to my shorthand classes. It was all I could do to keep up. I scarcely got a question in edgeways.

'I had a wonderful case the other day,' Doris went on. 'A Swedish woman came to see me absolutely distraught because her little son had drowned. As we were talking, I looked around and saw a small boy with blond hair and blue eyes standing in the room. He went up to the woman, laid his hand on her arm and smiling up into her face said: 'Love you Alskling, love you.'

When I told her, she burst into tears. 'That's my son,' she said, 'I could never be cross with him because whenever he was naughty, and I tried to tell him off, he used to come over, look at me with those big blue eyes and say 'Love you darling, love you.' Alskling is Swedish for darling.' When she left, she was a different woman. In fact, her husband was so delighted, he phoned later and asked for a sitting for himself.'

It seemed Doris could use her abilities in a variety of different ways. 'One woman asked me to visit her at home,' Doris explained, 'and amongst other things she wanted me to find out where her late husband's solid gold cigarette case had gone because it was very valuable. I'd never been in the place before, but I found myself walking straight to the wardrobe. Right at the back, I came across a dress suit. I took it out and there – in the pocket – was the lighter.'

But other ventures weren't so successful. 'Once I tried to help with a murder case,' she said, 'but all I kept getting in connection with the murderer was a load of sand. Sand everywhere. I didn't know what to make of it. Could he have thrown the murder weapon away in sand dunes, I wondered, but it was no use. I couldn't get anywhere. Then, later, when the killer was eventually caught, it turned out he was from Jordan – in the desert. It's all a matter of interpretation you see.'

Doris went on to explain how it all began.

She was born Doris Sutton in Grantham, Lincolnshire, the daughter of a Romany gypsy who left the road to become a blacksmith and raise a family. Perhaps she knew young Margaret Thatcher, who came from the same town, though it's unlikely they moved in similar circles – what with Margaret's father owning two shops and later becoming an Alderman, then Mayor, while Doris' dad was a simple blacksmith.

Apparently, Doris seemed a bit different right from the start. As a toddler, she explained, she played with a troupe of imaginary friends, including an exotic girl with dark skin called Pansy – though to her they weren't imaginary at all. They were real and solid, and she couldn't understand why no one else could see them. She also talked to people she could see walking around; people who her parents insisted had recently died.

'There's something strange about our Doris,' her down to earth, non-Romany mother would complain to Doris' father Sam – as well she might. But Sam, who was probably psychic himself seemed to understand. Doris he reckoned, was just fine the way she was.

Doris adored her father, and they had a very close bond. His kindly words of wisdom and caring philosophy remained with her all her life. She was devastated when he died when she was only 13. But in the years that followed, it never occurred to her she might have inherited some of his Romany powers. It was only when war broke out, and Doris became a driver in the air force, that the first hints began to show.

'We didn't have much money for entertainment in those days,' she said, 'so quite often we'd go to the 'spook show' – our name for the local Spiritualist church. Frequently the medium would point to me and say: 'One of these days you'll be doing this.' and I'd just laugh.

'When we got back to the billet I'd wrap a towel around my head and muck about, going 'Wooooo...!!!' and pretending to give the girls messages. They'd say, 'That's right! It's true,' but I thought they were just playing along.'

Then early one morning she was asked to drive her officer to an air-strip just before a big operation. 'I was standing on the edge of the field, dawn was about to break, and there was a deathly hush,' she recalled. 'Suddenly I noticed a very young man, a rear-gunner walking towards his plane. He was whistling 'The Lord's My Shepherd' and as I watched, I found I was crying. Tears were running down my face. He was so young and I just knew, with absolute certainty, he wasn't coming back. I was right. He was killed that morning.'

But, of course, young airmen were tragically killed so frequently in those years; Doris put her feelings down to coincidence rather than a premonition.

It was only later when personal tragedy struck, and Doris saw her late father walk into the room – 'As real and solid as when he was alive...'– to tell her to be prepared, that she began to think perhaps there might be something in what those old mediums at the spook show had said after all.

The stories flowed out of Doris; some touching, some humorous. It was clear she'd lived a varied and fascinating life and suffered her share of sadness – losing her longed-for baby son when he was only a few months old – as well as battling frequent bouts of serious ill health herself. And now here she was, dispensing comfort to the bereaved, who seemed to find her phone number despite the fact that Doris didn't advertise. 'Someone got in touch the other day after overhearing two ladies talking about me on holiday in Rome!' said Doris, shaking her head in amazement.

These days she seldom saw spirits, she explained. After an unfortunate incident some years before, in which she got up in the middle of the night to visit the bathroom and saw the dark figure of a man skulking in the shadows. Terrified, Doris screamed, thinking it was an intruder, only for the figure to disappear before her eyes at her shrieks.

'Since then, I rarely see them,' she said, 'I'm mainly clairaudient these days – I hear their voices.'

I listened enthralled, my notebook almost full. It seemed to me a feature about this Doris Fisher Stokes would make a fine opening to the supernatural series. (Incidentally, although she became famous as Doris Stokes – throughout her married life she'd been Mrs Fisher Stokes. The name was only later shortened by her publishers because it was a bit too long to fit the design of the paperback cover. Doris told me once that the long name arose because her husband John had been adopted and he decided to use both his birth name and adoptive parents' name, together.)

And so we galloped through Doris's colourful early life until we were more or less back to the present day. I was more than happy that I'd got enough material for the feature. I started to close my book. But...

'And now,' said Doris, 'I'll do a sitting for you.'

I was alarmed. I realised I'd been rather nervous about this meeting. Ghost stories were one thing, but I didn't actually want to come into contact with any real-life examples thank you very much. Doris' friendly, entertaining manner had lulled my fears, but now they snapped back.

'Oh no, that's not necessary,' I said hastily, making to pack my notebook away. After all, I was very young. I hadn't lost anyone close. There was no one I wanted to get in touch with.

'But it is necessary,' Doris insisted. 'Anyone can say they can do these things and it could be a pack of lies. I have to prove to you that I'm telling the truth.'

And before I could protest, she'd begun.

To my relief, she didn't draw the curtains or darken the room or light incense or mess about lighting candles. She just settled more comfortably in her chair, took another puff on her cigarette and began chatting to a person I couldn't see. It was rather like watching someone having a phone conversation, only without a visible phone and with the caller a long way off, on a line that kept breaking up. 'I've got a man here who passed with a heart attack,' she said.

I must have turned rather pale because she added quickly, 'It's not your father love. He's still here with us on the earth plane.'

Then she began to cough, a terrible cough from the bottom of her lungs. 'He was coughing,' she said, 'and I'm getting the letter 'M'.'

I was completely puzzled. The only relation I could think of, who'd passed away, was my grandfather, my father's father. And his initial was 'A'. He hadn't had a heart attack either.

'Well my husband's name is Michael,' I suggested.

Doris looked confused. 'No, no that's not it. Now he's saying he loves brass bands... and he's met Gertie.'

Nope. Still a complete blank.

Doris looked puzzled, but she ploughed on. There were more names I couldn't place, but I scribbled them all down anyway. Then, 'He says there's two rooms in your house without carpet, and he likes the yellow and orange flowers.'

Now, this was odd. Recently married, I'd just moved into a new home where there were indeed two rooms with bare boards on the floor while we saved up for carpet. Also, just a few days earlier, we'd bought an eye-catching new duvet cover – in the trendy '70s style – ablaze with orange and yellow flowers to brighten up the spare room.

'And they're talking about Phyllis,' Doris continued. 'There's been a bit of worry about Phyllis lately and she's been to the hospital for tests but she's ok.'

Odder still. Phyllis was the birth name of a relative who'd changed it to something she considered more glamorous, years before. Very few people knew she'd been christened Phyllis. Plus, she had indeed just been to the hospital for tests, but the results were not yet back.

'Now that was the name Wyn,' Doris continued, 'and Joy. And then that was Len.'

'Yes I know them,' I admitted.

'And Paul,' said Doris, 'and in connection with Paul, the name Clark. And they're singing happy birthday to Paul, so I know his birthday is just coming or just gone. How old's Paul going to be love?' This last question was to the invisible speaker, not me.

'They're showing me four candles on a cake,' Doris went on, 'so I know he's going to be four.'

I was astonished. Before I arrived, Doris hadn't even known I was married, but Joy was my sister-in-law, her husband Len, Len's mother was called Wyn, and their little boy was named Paul. Their surname was Clark and Paul's fourth birthday would arrive in two weeks' time.

After such a slow start this seemed impressive.

And, in fact, the sitting was more impressive than I realised at the time. Visiting my mother a few days later, I found I'd still got my notebook in my bag.

'So what did the medium say?' Mum asked when I told her what I'd been doing.

'Oh, most of it was wrong,' I said, 'but there were some intriguing bits.' I started to read back my shorthand.

'She was going on about a man who died of a heart attack, with a terrible cough. And the letter 'M'.'

My mother's jaw dropped. 'Well, that's my father,' she said. 'He had bronchitis, and he died of a heart attack during a fit of coughing. His name was Martin.'

I'd completely forgotten about my other grandfather; because he died when I was such a small child, I hardly remembered him. It turned out he adored brass bands and his sister – who passed away years before I was born – was called Gertie. The other names that meant nothing to me were members of his family, long estranged.

All the things I'd told Doris were wrong, were actually 100% right. What's more, that day we got the news that Phyllis' test results had come back and she was fine.

Over the years that followed, many critics were to claim that Doris was a fake; that she guessed details or threw out a series of common but random names until grief-stricken clients recognised one and desperately tried to fit things to their own circumstances. They said Doris milked the bereaved for information and then fed it back to them. They said Doris must research her clients' backgrounds in advance, then present the details to them as if coming from the spirit world.

Yet, in my case, not one of those tactics would have been possible. I was not desperate to contact anyone. In fact, I was actively averse to a reading and tried to avoid one. I gave Doris no help whatsoever. Just the opposite. I did not fill in any extra details for her to feed back to me. I wasn't needy, and I was too busy scribbling notes.

What's more, as a journalist in the days before the internet I know how difficult it was to research people's backgrounds. That's what I did for a living, and it wasn't easy – particularly if the person concerned was an ordinary member of the public who'd never been mentioned in the press.

With just two hours' notice, only my maiden name to go on – I was not at that point using my married name – and unaware I was married or where I lived, it would have been impossible for Doris to discover the names of my in-laws and their extended family or the exact age of their son, or guess correctly the state of a relative's health, using her little-known birth name. These were things that even my closest friends were unlikely to have known. Not because they were secrets but because they didn't feature strongly in my day to day life at that point.

By the time the sitting ended, I was baffled. It was very difficult to imagine my grandfather (or anyone else for that matter) having been in the room. I had no sense of an unseen presence whatsoever. I heard nothing, saw nothing, and experienced not so much as a single goosebump. Yet there seemed to be no explanation for what Doris had just done. Even if she'd been reading my mind and been able to access things I'd long forgotten, she couldn't have discovered the results of a test that hadn't arrived yet.

I had no doubt that this unusual Mrs Fisher Stokes could do something most of us can't.

So, Doris went back to her tea and her cigarettes. We chatted about the series, when it might appear in the magazine, whether Doris should have her hair done again before our photographer arrived to take her picture, and what other subjects she thought might make good themes for part two. Then it was time to go, and Doris led me back to the front door. She started to open it, then stopped.

'I'll tell you how you can earn some money to buy carpet for those two rooms,' she said suddenly.

'How's that?' I laughed.

'You can write my book for me. Someone else tried a while ago, but it never came to anything.'

On the magazine, we frequently ran ghosted human interest stories, so I'd written quite a few, but I'd never attempted anything as long as a book. Interviewees would often tell me at the end of a meeting, 'You could write a book about my life!' and they were nearly always wrong – their experiences, interesting though they were, were seldom substantial enough to fill a whole book. But in Doris' case, it was obvious her story was packed full of incident. I sensed that, for once, this was a narrative that could stay the course.

Despite this, I didn't think a book about Doris would ever be published. Most autobiographies on sale then seemed to be by people who were famous. They were movie stars or mountain-climbers or top sportsmen, or they hobnobbed with royalty. This Mrs Fisher Stokes was a complete unknown. Worse, she was a spiritualist medium, and mediums were regarded with suspicion in the media and with deep disapproval by the church.

During our chat, Doris said she'd heard that at that time mediums were banned from appearing on the BBC, and it was little more than 30 years since a medium – Helen Duncan – was actually imprisoned under the Witchcraft Act in 1944. This act was actually repealed in 1951 – well it had been around since 1735 – but it was replaced with the Fraudulent Mediums Act which prohibited anyone from claiming to be a psychic medium while attempting to deceive and make money from the deception.

I'd certainly never heard of a medium demonstrating publicly outside of a spiritualist meeting – though perhaps they did. And the only time you seemed to read about them in the press was when one or another was exposed as a fraud.

In such a climate, I could see no way that Doris' book would ever find a publisher. Clearly, no one would ever read this story. And I would never be reimbursed for my efforts – let alone earn enough to buy a piece of carpet because Doris certainly couldn't afford to pay me anything.

And yet... I'd always wanted to write a book, and it was a good story. Could I do it, I wondered?

'Ok,' I heard myself saying, 'let's give it a go!'

Insane or what?

CHAPTER 2

Deep in rural Essex, yet surprisingly close to Stansted Airport, the taxi suddenly swung off the main road into a leafy country lane and then on into a long, long drive through parkland.

Doris was leaning forward eagerly in her seat. 'This is it, nearly there,' she said, though there was nothing to be seen but trees. Then we rounded a bend and astonishingly, a vast, red-brick Jacobean-style mansion was spread out in front of us; rows and rows of intricate chimneys and ornate finials lined up against the sky.

So this was perhaps Britain's strangest educational establishment – the Arthur Findlay College.

Doris' irreverent younger self might well have dubbed it the 'School for Spooks' but, at the time, it was officially known as a college for psychic studies. Or, as our magazine headline writers put it later: the School for Psychics.

Stansted Hall was to feature as part two of our supernatural series. Doris' idea. 'You ought to include Stansted Hall, luvvie,' she said, when I explained that we hadn't yet decided what to include in parts two and three. 'There's nothing else like it,' she added.

And as Doris knew many of the staff, she offered to come along and introduce me. 'I don't get out much,' she said, 'and it would be nice to have a day in the country.'

It was fine by me. Doris was good company and it could be helpful if she knew her way around the place.

As the car crunched across the gravel forecourt and pulled up in front of a massive oak door, I could see Doris' instincts had been right. Under a glowering sky, or looming through the fog on a winters' night, atmospheric Stansted

Hall could have doubled as the location for a vampire movie. In fact, it so looked the part, you could almost criticise the location as too clichéd. Yet there was no doubt about it, the building would be the perfect illustration for our series.

The imposing front door led into big, oak-panelled rooms with mullioned windows looking out over a four-acre lawn and swaying horse chestnuts. Yet, somehow, the place didn't feel creepy. Cheerful people were bustling everywhere. Around 50 adult students were in residence, taking time off from day-to-day lives for short courses on everything from healing and mediumship to psychic art and auras. Beneath the chatter, a sense of quiet expectation and anticipation filled the air. The people who came here were clearly searching for something.

'There's a demonstration just starting,' said manager Paul Gibson when the introductions were over, 'Want to see it?'

He led Doris and me into the library where a group of students was sitting around a large table which had been set up with a bowl of water, a pack of clay, and various modelling tools. Margaret Mills Muntz, a grandmother and retired teacher from Ohio, USA was opening the clay.

'I wasn't planning to be doing this,' said Margaret, peeling back the wrappings. 'I'm only here on a three-week visit as a student, but they found out I could do psychic modelling, so they got me to show them!'

It was all a bit of a novelty to Margaret herself too, because until four years earlier she hadn't been aware she possessed any artistic talent whatsoever.

'I was busy teaching and running the school library,' she said, 'but then I started suffering from arthritis, and someone suggested I try psychic healing. So I had a session and in passing, while working on my arthritis, the medium mentioned I had the ability to model with clay.'

This was news to Margaret and sounded highly unlikely. She reckoned she'd never had an artistic bone in her body. But for some reason the words stuck in her mind. Months later, on impulse, she bought some clay. To her surprise, she liked the smooth, cool feel of the material on her fingers. Absent-mindedly she began working it, almost like dough, without really knowing what she was supposed to do. Then, suddenly, within just a few minutes, she realised the face, head and shoulders of what was recognisably an elderly man had somehow formed in the clay before her eyes.

'I liked him so much I kept him and asked a psychic friend to do a reading for me,' said Margaret, 'I was told the man was a doctor, and in a past life I'd served with him in France as his nurse – and a little bit more!'

Margaret quickly found that although she never knew what she was making until it was finished, she was able to create similar models for other people. And, oddly, these little figures usually turned out to be relevant to the recipient. Frustratingly though, Margaret was unable to do the psychic interpretations herself.

'So that's why I came to Stansted Hall,' she explained. 'I want to learn more so I can do the readings myself.' She paused and picked up a ball of clay. 'Here,' she said, 'take this and hold it in your hands for a few minutes. Your vibrations will go into the clay.'

Obediently, I took the sticky lump and held it between my palms for a while. I didn't feel a thing vibration-wise, but after a few minutes Margaret seemed satisfied. She took it back and then her busy fingers began kneading and pinching, moulding and shaping, while the surrounding students craned closer to see what was happening.

Then, abruptly, it was over. Margaret stopped, leaned back from the clay and there in front of her – no more than three inches high – was the head and shoulders of what, judging by the turned up corners of her head-gear, appeared to be a little Dutch woman. She was charming, but I didn't recognise her. 'Never mind,' said Margaret. 'She could be one of your ancestors, or your spirit guide. Come back later when she's dry and you can take her home.'

Secretly disappointed my guide wasn't Cleopatra or some equally glamorous type, I returned to the hall. Outside, a psychic artist was demonstrating her work, there were lectures on mediumship going on, and in the Blue Room – with its walls of delicate Wedgewood – a healing session was in progress.

Some of the students, though, were just chilling in easy-chairs over cups of coffee. 'I came here for a rest,' said Liz, a 32 year old housewife from Brighton. 'It looked like a lovely place, and I thought that learning about a fascinating subject at the same time would be a rest in itself.'

So was she enjoying herself? 'I'm loving it!' said Liz.

Just then, Doris came over with a tall, imposing figure with white hair and an air of authority. Doris was very seldom overawed by anyone but she looked a little nervous in the presence of this man. I realised this must be Gordon Higginson – the president of the Spiritualists National Union which owned Stansted Hall. Doris regarded him as a great man.

A medium almost since boyhood, and son of medium Fanny Higginson, Gordon from Longton (near Stoke on Trent), had apparently been demonstrating his abilities in spiritualist churches since the age of 12. Known back then as the Boy Wonder, and later, Mr Mediumship, Gordon was immensely versatile and had mastered most of the psychic arts. It was said he could even go into a trance and produce ectoplasm – some sort of foamy substance that would shape itself into a likeness of the departed spirit – a feat regarded by fellow spiritualists as possibly the most difficult of them all.

This was a gift Doris herself had never possessed, she explained. She greatly admired anyone who could do it and was fascinated by this curious ability. From her description though, it sounded rather alarming. 'Once, during a séance, something went wrong,' Doris told me on the way down in the taxi, 'Gordon was wearing a belt and he was left with great red wheals around his waist where the buckle burned him.'

As well as his mystical powers, Gordon was also a talented manager. When he took on Stansted Hall, it was rumoured the place was in debt and the sprawling Victorian structure starting to crumble, but Gordon was successfully raising funds and returning the old place to its former glory.

Yet, despite all these qualities, our encounter today was a bit delicate. Just a few weeks before, Gordon had been denounced in a national newspaper as a fraud. He was accused of faking ectoplasm. In a darkened room it was claimed, Gordon had taken advantage of the dim light to pass off a piece of gauzy white cloth as a supernatural manifestation. The story had appeared in the press and – awkward as it was – it was a subject I couldn't ignore today.

Gordon didn't exactly roll his eyes when I finally dared to raise the matter, but he was still clearly distressed about the episode.

'What they said was totally untrue,' he insisted. 'The 'evidence' was from a man who attended a séance four years before. He claimed to have climbed in through a window and found a space under a chair which contained white fabric that he said was used to fake the ectoplasm. Well just look at these chairs...'

We'd reached one of the rooms in which séances were held and Gordon picked up a chair and turned it upside down.

It was made of wood with a padded seat, but there didn't seem to be any room for a secret compartment. 'How could you hide anything under there? And look at the windows! How could he get through?'

I took in the heavy sash frames and the locks on the inside.

'It wouldn't be very easy to open one of these from the outside and climb in,' Gordon went on. 'And even if he managed it, why did he wait four years to say anything?'

So what about the belt buckle incident that Doris mentioned?

'Someone had set up a tape recorder near me during the séance,' said Gordon, 'and they'd plugged it into the light socket. I was wearing a belt with a metal buckle and for some reason it suddenly became red hot. When the doctor examined me afterwards, he discovered I'd got third-degree burns. I don't know why it happened. It seems to be something to do with having electrical apparatus nearby. Ectoplasm is a vapour produced by the body. For some reason, light and electrical currents focussed on the medium when ectoplasm's being produced has a bad effect.'

Gordon decided to take a break from ectoplasm for a while after that – and who could blame him?

Sadly for Gordon, there were to be more accusations of fraud over the years that followed. Yet, he was greatly respected by many devoted followers who reckoned he was one of the best mediums around. There's no doubt he worked very hard to make Stansted Hall and the Arthur Findlay College a success.

My visit was almost at an end. Gordon returned to his presidential duties and, while we waited for the taxi to take us home, Doris sank gratefully into one of the easy chairs in the Great Hall while I moved to the other end to do a last interview with another student.

After a bit, I glanced up, and noticed Doris was no longer alone. A man I hadn't seen before had pulled up a seat next to hers and they were deep in conversation. What's more, the man appeared to be recording what Doris was saying. Alarmed that perhaps another journalist was covering the same story – in which case I could be in big trouble back at the office – I brought my interview to a rapid close and (as casually as possible) moved across to see what was going on.

'Oh hello luv,' said Doris, 'won't be long. I had to talk to this man. I saw him walking upstairs and then I heard his wife say: 'Will you have a word with my husband? He's ever so upset'.'

It turned out that the man had lost his wife, and since her death had been desperately looking for proof of an afterlife. He'd visited mediums and spiritualist churches without any luck and he'd vowed to make one last attempt. He would spend a week at Stansted Hall and if he drew a blank, he said, he'd give up forever.

That particular day was his last day. There'd been no message and, when Doris saw him, he was just on his way upstairs to pack.

'When she started coming out with these messages, I went back for my tape recorder,' the man explained.

I sat down and listened quietly as Doris went on to describe the appearance of his late wife and also of the couple's only son who'd passed away six months after his mother.

By this time the man was in tears. Silently, he took out his wallet and with a shaking hand produced a snapshot of his lost family. The smiling faces were exactly as Doris had described.

'Now, she's telling me about a special date, that's important,' Doris continued. 'September 26th. Is that your anniversary love?' she was talking to the wife, 'No?' Doris turned back to the husband, 'She says no, it's more important than that. You used to celebrate the day you met. September 26th.'

The man nodded. 'That's right. That was when we met and it always seemed more important to us than our wedding anniversary.'

There had been no prompting, no incorrect names, and the man was practically too overcome to speak, let alone provide Doris with details. What's more, Doris knew that her part of the magazine series had already been written; so as far as she could tell, this encounter would never be known to anyone other than the two of them.

By the time she'd finished, the widower was a changed man. He kissed her cheek gratefully and practically bounded up the stairs to pack. His visit to Stansted Hall hadn't been in vain after all.

A few minutes later, our taxi arrived but as we made our way to the main door I heard a voice calling me back. It was Margaret Muntz and she was holding the little model she'd made for me – now dry and also painted.

'Here she is, all finished,' she said. 'The medium said she's your spirit guide and she's a nun.'

This was possibly even more disappointing. Even further from Cleopatra than a regular Dutch woman. But she was charming nevertheless and a kind gift – though privately I had my doubts about her being a nun because Margaret had been inspired to paint her outfit pale blue, and I'd only ever seen nuns wearing black.

Years later, I was to discover that some nuns do, in fact, wear just the shade of blue that Margaret chose but for now, I put the odd little model in my bag and forgot about her.

CHAPTER 3

Back in London, part two of the series was written and photographed, and Doris and I began to discuss how we were going to put together her autobiography. The logistics were tricky as I had a full-time job on the opposite side of London from Fulham, and lived nearly 60 miles away on the massive building site that was the embryo new town of Milton Keynes – still minus its shopping centre, hospital, railway station, and just about everything else.

The MK Development Corporation liked to refer to the place romantically as: 'The City of Trees' – though, at the time, the City of Dead Trees' would have been more apt; the forests of spindly sticks they planted on every verge were left unwatered and died in their thousands.

Meanwhile, in the press, the town-to-be was ridiculed as 'The city of Concrete Cows' on account of a whimsical artwork created by the 'artist in residence' as a community project. Apparently, the two cows, two calves, and a bullock were actually constructed from scrap metal, chicken wire, old newspaper, and fibre-glass rather than concrete. But when they were seen 'grazing' in a local park, the press drew their own hilarious conclusions.

'Well it's too far for you to come over here from up there every time luvvie,' said Doris who wisely made no comment on the concrete cows, though I'm sure she thought I lived somewhere odd. 'Maybe we can tape it.'

We ended up settling on a monthly series of interviews in her flat, combined with cassette tapes that Doris would record in her spare time and send to me by post, plus supplementary questions over the phone. It was a long process, but bit by bit it began to come together.

As far as I was concerned, the book was still very much a light-hearted, weekend 'hobby'. I didn't take it too seriously. On the magazine, life was busy and we were enjoying a brief moment of high excitement. The Queen, no less, was coming to pay us a visit and Doris was eager to hear all about it.

We didn't realise it at the time, but we were witnessing the first stirrings of the total transformation of our shabby slice of London. The previous year, 1977, had been the Queen's Silver Jubilee and during the celebrations, some distance upriver from us, the Queen had opened a welcome patch of waterside greenery named in her honour: the Jubilee Gardens. In truth, at the time, they weren't much more than a large area of lawn between Hungerford and Westminster Bridges. These days they're an ideal spot from which to watch the great wheel of the London Eye slowly turning, but back then they were just a vast improvement on the scruffy car park they replaced. They were quickly pounced on by sun-starved office workers to top up their tans in their lunch hours – us magazine reporters included.

How many of us – hungrily tucking into our Ryvita and cottage-cheese sandwiches in the vain hope of saving a few calories in order to enjoy a Mars Bar later – realised that 25 years before, this had been the site of the famous Festival of Britain? Or that we were, in fact, sprawling on the exact spot where the once-futuristic Dome of Discovery wowed the crowds in 1951, and the 300 foot high, cigar-shaped Skylon cast a pencil shadow over the tarmac.

I, for one, had no idea. I'd never even heard of the Festival of Britain. The Queen, of course, would have remembered. She was there. She and her husband Prince Philip toured the Festival site one chilly May day when she was still just young, carefree Princess Elizabeth. The couple even attended the inaugural concert at the newly-built Festival Hall.

As we got closer to the big day, our building was soon being painted, polished, and prettified (well, as best you can with a brutal slab of dour concrete). On the great day, the entire magazine staff, dressed in our best, lined the corridor as the Editor conducted Her Majesty through our spookily tidy departments. Unfortunately, the more senior staff who naturally had the best positions at the front of the crowd happened to be quite tall, so squashed near the back, I could only snatch tantalising glimpses of the Queen over shoulders and through arms. Nevertheless, I got a fleeting impression of a small, slim figure in pale pastel with matching pastel hat, looking amazingly young, as she glided slowly by… and then she was gone.

We didn't see him but in another part of the building, the Duke of Edinburgh was also touring magazines. Apparently he paused in the offices of Cheeky Weekly (how could he not?), a children's comic destined to be sadly short-lived, which at the time encouraged young readers to send the Editor their favourite jokes. Stopping by a desk, the Duke impulsively picked up a letter from the reader mailbag and opened it. 'Heard the one about the Irish bookworm?' read the Duke out loud, 'It was found dead in a brick.'

Probably borderline illegal these days but it tickled Prince Philip. He moved on, chuckling.

Doris thought it was hilarious when I told her the following week. It seemed a shame she couldn't have been there. Celebrities, Royals, she loved to hear about their lives. Oddly enough, a few years later, that same magazine was to invite Doris to a carol concert at Westminster Abbey attended by Princess Diana, the Princess of Wales.

Doris was thrilled and relished every minute, but afterwards her abiding memory was not the singing or the spectacular Abbey, but concern for the Princess. 'That child was so thin,' she said. 'I've never seen anyone so thin. I'm worried about her.'

Much later, it was said that the Princess was very unhappy at this point. Whether Doris picked up on it or not, she didn't say, but it was obvious she sensed trouble ahead.

As well as her private readings, Doris also ran a development class for aspiring mediums. It was held every Tuesday evening in a small room at Fulham Town Hall, just up the road from her flat. The class was free. The only cost for Doris' pupils was a whip-round at the end to pay for the room hire. It sounded intriguing so, one night, I went along with Doris to see what it was all about.

As we approached the town hall, we found a little knot of would-be psychics – both men and women – gathered outside on the pavement waiting for Doris to arrive. They greeted her eagerly and we all went inside. There was a lot of laughter and friendly banter as we found the room and settled ourselves around the big horseshoe-shaped wooden table with Doris at the head. After a few jokes to relax us all, Doris got everyone to join hands, close their eyes, and meditate quietly.

'You see everyone's psychic,' she explained to me. 'We've all got the spark, but it just needs bringing out in most people.'

As the fledglings attempted to 'tune in', Doris watched them with a motherly air. Every now and then she'd turn to one and ask what they were seeing or hearing. Then she'd help them make sense of their impressions.

'My guide Ramanov tells me when one of them's getting something,' she explained afterwards. 'Most of them are here because they've had sittings with me in the past, and became so interested they wanted to do it themselves.'

She wouldn't accept just anyone into the class though.

'I always ask them why they want to be a medium,' she said. 'If they say to make money, I won't have them. That's not what it's about. It's service, not selfishness.'

The hour passed quickly and, at the end, the students seemed reluctant to leave. They clustered around, each one hoping to exchange a few words with Doris. By the time she managed to extricate herself, it was getting late and she was looking forward to getting home for her standard pick-me-up – a cup of tea and a cigarette in front of the TV.

Yet there were even more aspects to Doris' work, I discovered. She was also a regular 'resident medium' at the SAGB – the HQ of the Spiritualist Association of Great Britain, at the time located in an elegant Georgian building in Belgrave Square, London. Members of the public could book a sitting with whichever accredited medium was on 'duty' that day, then wander through the gleaming black entrance doors of number 33, admire the ornate period plasterwork and graceful staircase, and even take a peek at the chair where Sir Arthur Conan Doyle (himself an ardent spiritualist), sat to pen his Sherlock Holmes stories.

The chair was bought at auction by the SAGB after the great man died, apparently. In truth, the heavily carved mahogany seat looked a tad knobbly and uncomfortable a perch for an author to sit on for hours on end, writing – but who knows? Sir Arthur, once ships' doctor on a whaling boat and also volunteer army doctor in the Boer War was clearly a tough fellow.

Back then, in the '70s, the late Tom Johanson – himself a renowned healer and medium – was head of the SAGB where Doris worked and he explained how she came to get the job. It was all a bit of an accident, it seems. As General Secretary of the Association, Tom was often asked to speak at spiritualist churches around the country and several years before, he'd been invited to address the church in Morecambe.

'When I arrived, they told me I should have been sharing the platform with one of their local mediums – a Doris Fisher Stokes,' said Tom, 'but unfortunately the arrangement had to be changed because Doris was very ill in hospital with breast cancer. She would be so disappointed to have missed me, they said.

'I'd never heard of this Doris, but I was sorry to hear she was so unwell. So, I offered to go and visit her in hospital the next morning. When we finally met, I must be honest and say that she looked so desperately ill in bed I didn't think she'd last the night. As a healer, I'm used to seeing very sick people and Doris looked about as bad as it's possible to get and still be here.

'Yet she seemed very pleased to see me. 'When I get well, can I come and work for you at the SAGB Tom?' she asked.

'I was so moved by her condition, how could I refuse? 'Of course you can!' I told her.

'What else could I say? But it was only to cheer her up. I didn't seriously think she'd last to the end of the week, let alone live long enough to come to London.

'Before I left, she asked me to give her healing, which of course I did.

'Doris you've got a job whenever you want it,' I promised as I left. Never dreaming for one second that she'd take me up on it. And that was the end of that. Or so I thought.'

If he ever heard of this Doris again, Tom assumed, it would probably be to read news of her passing away.

So, imagine his surprise when, a few months later, he looked up from his London desk to find Doris standing in front of him; bright, smiling and apparently radiant with health. Could this be a ghost, he must have wondered.

'I couldn't believe my eyes,' said Tom. 'I was absolutely amazed. The last time I'd seen Doris, I was certain she wasn't long for this world, yet now, here she was, right as rain. I had no idea she was coming. I had no idea she was still in this world, let alone in London. 'Well here I am,' she said, beaming. 'Ready to start.' And she insisted her remarkable recovery was all down to me and the healing I'd given her!'

Tom was delighted Doris was so well of course but, privately, somewhat concerned. He was a man of his word, and he'd made a promise, but the SAGB had strict rules about the mediums they accepted.

'They have to provide references about their mediumship from six different spiritualist churches,' he said, 'and then go through a demonstration, under test conditions for us here at head office. Doris had done none of these things – and I couldn't very well ask her to now. So, I bent the rules. It wasn't that I had a sixth sense she was good. I had no idea. I'd never seen her work. But she'd just come through a very serious illness; she was so excited and full of hope, I couldn't go back on my promise.'

So Tom put her on the books there and then. It was an act of kindness, nothing more.

Soon the reports started coming in.

'Every medium gets a few bad reports and so did Doris,' said Tom, 'but she also got a great many good ones. After a while, people weren't just pleased with their sittings; they were writing letters asking us to let them know when she was coming back.

'I noticed that when she was working for a group on a platform she was a natural. Where some mediums are performers, and can't disguise the fact they like to be the centre of attention, Doris would get up there and just chat to people as if they were in her living room. She smiled down benevolently on everyone, and people just warmed to her.

'As the months passed, I began to realise that this lady I'd accepted out of kindness, was really something quite special.'

I could see exactly what he meant. The more I found out about Doris, and the more I followed her around, the more I realised Tom was right. Everywhere we went, though she was still more or less unknown, people seemed to gravitate to Doris and she had a smile and a kind word for them all.

It was fascinating. I was still convinced, however, that no one would ever read the book we were developing – apart from Doris and her friends of course. And I wasn't alone. I told very few people what I was doing, but the ones I did tell weren't exactly encouraging. 'Why on earth are you wasting your time?' was the typical response. 'No one's going to publish that.'

And, of course, I agreed. But that wasn't the point. As far as I was concerned, it was an experiment and I was enjoying it!

CHAPTER 4

It was quite early in the morning when the phone rang.

'Guess what?' said Doris' in a chirpy voice as I stumbled blearily to answer. Though we often caught up over the phone with extra details for the book, it was unusual for her to call first thing. She sounded excited. 'We're going to Australia! John and me.'

'Australia?' As far as I knew Doris had never even been out of the country before, let alone contemplated a trip to the other side of the world. And the last time John was abroad was probably when he was a paratrooper, dropped over Arnhem in the Netherlands, during World War II.

'Yes! Remember that Australian TV crew that came to see me the other week?'

I vaguely recalled Doris mentioning a documentary maker from Australia, who'd popped in recently, and done a bit of filming in her flat.

'Well, apparently it came out well. They thought it was so interesting they've invited me over to appear on one of their chat shows. The Don Lane Show it's called. They're flying us both out there! John and me. And they're going to put us up in a hotel!'

Doris was thrilled. 'I wonder what I should pack? It's hot over there isn't it?'

I was amazed. How odd that in the UK no one outside the spiritualist movement seemed interested in talking to Doris, who was on their doorstep – yet this Australian TV company reckoned it was worthwhile to fly her halfway around the world for a few minutes on screen. 'That's fantastic Doris!' I said. 'When are you off?'

'Quite soon I think,' she said. 'We've got to get passports and what-not. And as it's such a long way, they say we can stay for two weeks.'

This was a very big deal for Doris. At this point, at nearly 60 years of age, as well as being a wife to John and mum to their adopted son Terry, her life had consisted mainly of working as a nurse in a mental hospital and demonstrating mediumship in the local spiritualist churches in her spare time, for around ten bob (50p) a session. The fee was little more than her bus fare home.

Night after night, as she stood at those chilly bus shelters, often in pouring rain, Doris would smile ruefully to herself and reflect that while the evening had been satisfying, you couldn't exactly call it glamorous. You certainly wouldn't take on that sort of work for the money or the glory!

Yet now, incredibly, here she was about to be whisked away on a plane and put up in a fancy hotel – just like those jet-setters she was always reading about in her Sun or Daily Mirror. It didn't seem real. Any moment, she felt, she'd surely wake up and find herself still marooned at some freezing request-stop in the back of beyond, hoping she hadn't missed the last bus home.

Yet, of course, the trip was true. It was really happening and once again Tony Ortzen of Psychic News was the catalyst. Back then, the paper was 'go-to' central for all media enquiries of a supernatural nature, so when an Australian TV crew wanted to make a show about paranormal phenomena in the old country, Psychic News was the first place they turned.

'They got in touch just like you did,' said Tony, 'and asked if I could recommend a psychic to film. By this time your magazine story had come out and the Doris interview seemed to work well. Also, by this time, I'd met Doris face to face myself. Straight off she said to me: 'You're a twin aren't you?' Not many people know that, and I'd certainly never mentioned it to her, but it's true. I've got a twin sister. Anyway, Doris struck me as so chatty and approachable she'd be perfect on camera.'

So that was how the Australian TV crew came to lug their cameras, lights, and film paraphernalia across London and up to the unlikely setting of Doris' modest flat amidst the flapping washing lines. And Tony was right. Doris did prove to be a natural – completely relaxed and unselfconscious on camera. 'It'll either work or it won't,' she told the producer. 'The cameras won't make any difference.' Fortunately, it seemed to work. In fact, as well as messages for the producer, Doris even had a few words with the grandmother of the cameraman as he was filming, which startled him no end. We never did see the resulting footage but evidently it was very intriguing; sometime later, Doris and John were winging their way to Melbourne and the studios of Channel 9 TV.

This was very exciting, of course, but I don't think any of us expected the trip to be anything more than the chance of a wonderful free holiday, with a cosy little chat in a studio thrown in. We'd never heard of this Don Lane or his show and assumed it must be some minor, little-watched day-time TV programme.

'It's a terribly long flight,' Tony warned Doris before she left. 'Never mind,' she said happily, though she'd probably never even been on a plane before, despite watching so many from the ground as a WAAF. "I'll take a sleeping pill. And anyway – maybe it'll make a nice chapter for the book.'

Maybe it would. And since I was still busy with my full-time day job on the magazine and working on Doris' tapes and transcripts at weekends, I reckoned I could probably take advantage of her absence to ease up a bit. To be honest, progress – on my battered electric typewriter complete with carbon paper and Tipp-Ex – was slow. But then, since no one actually wanted the book, except Doris herself of course, there was no rush. It was more of a hobby really. What harm would there be in my having a little holiday too? I thought.

All was quiet for a week or so and then, out of the blue, came another phone call. Over a crackly line, Doris sounded quite breathless. 'We won't be back yet after all,' she said. 'We're staying on, for SIX WEEKS! It's all gone a bit mad here. Kerry Packer's sending me on tour – all round the country. And everyone's saying I should write a book. I've told them I have. Is it nearly finished?'

Gulp. I was probably just about on Chapter 5 at this point.

'Um, nearly,' I fibbed – which probably didn't fool Doris one bit. But, at least if she was away for six weeks, I'd got time to make sure it was ready for when she got back. Yet, I was confused.

Back then – in the days before the internet, emails, mobile phones, and even texts – it wasn't easy to find out what was going on, on the other side of the world. Where Kerry Packer fitted into all this, I had no idea. I'd heard of him. He was often in the news at that time, but wasn't he something to do with cricket and cricket tours?

It was only later that I was able to piece together what happened. As well as being a big name in cricket circles, Kerry Packer was an Australian media tycoon who also happened to own the Channel 9 TV station.

As for this unknown Don Lane, it turned out he was an American-born singer and actor who now hosted the highest-rated variety show in Australian TV history. He was also, at the time, said to be the highest paid performer on Australian TV.

Doris had unwittingly stumbled into the spotlight on Australia's most popular and talked-about TV show.

Totally ignorant of all this, of course, Doris just pottered on being Doris, good-naturedly having a go at whatever anyone asked her to do. Once the cameras started rolling, as well as chatting with the charming Don himself ('Handsome boy. Lovely smile.'), Doris was encouraged to talk to the live studio audience and show them what she did. Such a demonstration wouldn't have been permitted on UK TV back then, I believe, but in Australia the same rules didn't seem to apply.

So Doris 'tuned in' just the way she always did on those endless evenings in the Spiritualist Church halls of the north, and it wasn't long before she was hearing her voices. Soon messages were pouring out to be claimed by members of the TV audience. Still jet-lagged, it was all a bit of a blur to Doris but one small exchange stood out in her mind. She was talking to a young girl in the audience about her grandfather. 'He says he drowned,' said Doris, 'and it's early morning but it's a bit puzzling because I can see a gun.'

'That's right,' said the girl. 'He was out duck shooting.'

The effect was electrifying. Don's show over-ran. At one point, the proceedings were wound up and Doris waved goodbye and returned to the dressing room to get changed, but no sooner had she taken off her 'rent a tent' evening dress as she called them, the production team rushed in to take her back to the studio for an encore. No one wanted her to stop. Eventually, when the programme finally came off air, the station switchboard went into meltdown with callers desperate to talk to Doris.

The next night, an episode of Starsky & Hutch (one of the top TV shows of the era), was postponed so that Doris could come back and do another lengthy live demonstration for Don in front of a new TV audience. 'And we didn't even do that for Sammy Davis Junior,' joked Don's producer.

When even this second appearance couldn't satisfy demand, Mike Edgeley, a top Australian tour promoter, approached Kerry Packer to suggest Doris go on a six-week tour around some of the country's biggest theatres.

The tour culminated with the Sydney Opera House which Doris filled three nights in a row. No wonder she sounded breathless. And in amongst all the theatre dates, there were wall-to-wall interviews with journalists and radio presenters, baffled by the fact their colleagues in the UK media could tell them nothing about this elderly Englishwoman who was such a sensation.

By the time Doris got home to London, she was exhausted but dazzled and understandably bemused. Her relaxing break had turned into an astonishing, whirlwind experience of a lifetime. Yet she'd only been doing what she'd always done for the last 30 years to almost complete indifference in England. How come the effect was so different in Australia? Inadvertently, she seemed to have become an antipodean household name. A celebrity. It was flattering but puzzling too.

Yet, back in London, none of us grasped the scale of what had happened on the other side of the world. We'd seen nothing and heard nothing. Over here, nothing had changed. Around Sir Oswald Stoll mansions, life quickly returned to normal. Doris was just that grey-haired woman with the slightly disabled husband on the second floor; the woman who did something a bit weird – fortune-telling or some such.

A trickle of journalists, intrigued by reports from friends in Australia of the Doris effect, began to wander over to Fulham to find out who she was, and how she did whatever it was she did. But apart from that, those six exhilarating weeks down-under seemed to have faded away like a glorious dream.

Then one day, Garth Pearce, show business editor of the Daily Express, happened upon the reports from abroad and was curious to meet Britain's unlikely and unknown overnight sensation.

He found the Stokes' unassuming flat, was welcomed in and – over tea and cigarettes – asked Doris dozens of questions. Soon, Garth found himself as beguiled as everyone else. He listened to Doris' reminiscences about the loss of her baby son, of receiving the letter telling her that her husband was missing (presumed dead) in the war, and of seeing her long-deceased father walk into the room – large as life – to say that her husband hadn't been killed and that he would return.

'You know you ought to write a book,' said Garth at last when Doris paused for breath.

'I have!' said Doris. 'I'll show you.'

By chance, the typed manuscript I'd hastily completed had arrived in the post just a few days before. Doris had probably not even finished reading it herself but, before Garth could protest, she hurried off to the bedroom and came back with the torn brown envelope.

'There it is!' she said putting it proudly on Garth's lap. 'What d'you think?'

Kind Garth politely skimmed a few chapters. Fortunately, he liked what he read. What's more, he'd recently written a novel himself, and he generously offered to introduce Doris to his agent: a dynamic young woman called Jenne Casarotto.

What we hadn't got at that stage was a title, though, and we couldn't send it off anywhere without one. We kicked around a few ideas but Doris couldn't make up her mind, so in the end, she called Psychic News for advice.

Once again it was Tony Ortzen who came to the rescue. 'I was busy and it wasn't top of my list of priorities,' recalled Tony, 'but not long afterwards, when I wasn't even thinking about it, the words: Voices in My Ear came into my head. As Doris was clairaudient – she heard voices rather than saw spirits – it seemed to sum up exactly how she worked.'

At the time, the trend was for short, punchy titles: The Shining, Star Wars, The Thornbirds, and so on, were big names of the era – so privately I wondered if this suggestion was quite cool enough. But Doris loved it and, of course, she was right. Voices in My Ear became the name of the manuscript. I quickly typed a new title page, and then we parcelled up our chunky heap of pages and sent them off to Garth's agent and also (a photocopy) to a publisher. To my astonishment and our joint delight, within a few weeks Voices was accepted by both.

And that, I thought was more or less that. It seemed to me extraordinarily lucky that the book had been accepted. The equivalent, today, of winning the lottery. Naturally, I was thrilled. But the story was told. It never occurred to me there might be more to say.

CHAPTER 5

'It seems like a very long time to wait,' said Doris. We'd just heard it would take around a whole year for Voices in My Ear to appear in the shops. Unused to the book world as we were, this seemed a bafflingly lengthy delay to us, but it was quite normal we were assured.

'Oh well,' said Doris philosophically, 'Ramanov says "just trust". They know what they're doing over there.' And by 'over there' she didn't mean the publisher's offices in Camberwell. The Spirit World worked in mysterious ways, as she was always telling me.

Ramanov was Doris' spirit guide. She wasn't sure how to spell his name and, at first, she had an idea he might originally be from Egypt but recently she'd got the feeling he was from Tibet. Not that it mattered much. These days, as far as Doris was concerned, he was just 'over there' keeping an eye on what she was up to 'down here'. Most nights, when everyone in the flat had gone to bed, the rooms quiet and the lights low, Doris said she tuned in and had a chat with him.

I got the impression of an odd kind of tutorial with an invisible but strict, old-fashioned professor. They'd review the events of Doris' day together; Doris would ask questions or voice her worries and Ramanov would apparently answer her and give her advice. He wasn't above ticking her off if he thought she'd behaved badly, and he could be snippy at times.

'Once I said to him, Ramanov, I don't understand all this business about having to love everybody. Some people I can't even like,' Doris told me once. 'And Ramanov said, you're not told to like them. You don't have to like them. You just have to love them.'

Doris never seemed to resent these pronouncements of Ramanov's and so now she settled down to wait for the book. Life went on much as before. Doris doing her sittings in the flat, plus helping out at the SAGB in Belgrave Square and at a few spiritualist churches in the area. She was also beginning to travel more, particularly overseas. While her Australian adventures attracted little attention in the UK, they'd not gone unnoticed in the USA and New Zealand. She was invited to take part in several TV and radio shows abroad.

When Voices finally hit the bookstalls in 1980, just after Doris' 60th birthday, it was a quiet affair. Doris was still more or less unknown in the UK. There was no big, publisher's launch. No fuss. Doris just threw a celebration party for friends and family at Wimbledon spiritualist church. The President of the church, Derek Robinson, a cheerful dynamo of a man who ran a greengrocer's stall in Brixton Market by day, had become a great friend since Doris and John arrived in London. Realising the Stokes' tiny flat was too small for such a get-together, he offered the church hall for the party. It was a fun evening with drinks and nibbles and good wishes and Doris proudly gave out copies of her book – now clad in a smart yellow cover with the name Doris Fisher Stokes beneath a professional portrait of Doris on the front. During the evening, she presented Tony Ortzen with an engraved identity bracelet in gold as a thank you for coming up with the title, and that – we thought – was probably that.

I don't think either of us was expecting anything more. Simply getting the book published seemed a momentous achievement.

Yet slowly, quietly, as the weeks passed, beneath the surface, things were happening. There was little publicity and no advertising yet like ripples in an invisible pond, word began to spread.

'D'you know your book's a best-seller?' said a friend one day, a few weeks later.

'What? No... What d'you mean?' I'd heard nothing about Voices since Doris' party.

'I was just in Smiths,' she said, 'and they've got this week's top ten books on a shelf in there and your Voices is one of the ten!'

'No!'

She must have been mistaken, of course, but I had to rush round to Smiths to see for myself. And there it was. Just inside the door. An island unit with the top ten books of the week displayed on shelves; and there, near the top – was it number two or three... (how can I not remember?) ...was the cheery yellow cover of Voices in My Ear.

I could hardly believe my eyes. It was so exciting. I stood back for a while to watch to see if anyone bought a copy (they didn't). I even surreptitiously spread a few copies out along the shelf to make them more eye-catching. Then, I dashed back home to phone Doris with the good news.

Soon there was talk of a reprint, even a sequel. People were clearly discovering the book and buying it. Occasionally, travelling home on the train after work, I'd see someone opposite with the familiar yellow volume in their hand, and I'd have to suppress the urge to rush over and ask if they were enjoying it.

Readers began recommending Voices to their friends, particularly friends who'd suffered a bereavement.

'You really must read this book by a woman called Doris Stokes, I was always being told,' recalled Christine Chambers from Hemel Hempstead in Hertfordshire. Christine's story was typical.

A few years before, aged just 19, Christine had tragically lost her teenage sweetheart in a motorcycle accident.

'Kevin was lovely,' says Christine. 'He had dark hair and the palest, bluest eyes you ever saw. We'd been together since we were 16. When he was 19, he saved up and bought me a beautiful engagement ring – a square cut diamond. My dad thought we were too young to get engaged, of course, but Kevin was training to be a printer and I was training to be a window-dresser, and we were quite certain that in a couple of years we'd have enough money to buy a house and get married.'

That summer, like young people all over the UK, Christine dared to go on one of the new, super-cheap package holidays that had just sprung up. Foreign travel wasn't just for the rich anymore. Suddenly, cut-price flights and bargain hotels were putting exotic destinations within reach of ordinary, everyday folk for the first time ever. Shiny, modern hotels like Lego blocks began to mushroom all around the Spanish Costas, and Christine was off to the brand new resort everyone was talking about – Benidorm.

Unfortunately, Kevin couldn't get the time off work so he stayed at home, but Christine promised to send him a postcard every day. She missed him, of course, but they were only going to be apart a week, and this trip was too good to miss.

'There were no mobile phones or internet in those days,' said Christine, 'so it was difficult for people to keep in touch. Even making a call to a foreign country on a landline was difficult and intimidating, particularly if you didn't speak the language.

'I had a great time in Benidorm, but I missed Kevin and I was looking forward to seeing him when I got home. I wondered if he'd like my glamorous Mediterranean tan and the giant sombrero I'd bought him. All the planes back to the UK from the Spanish resorts in those days were crammed with multi-coloured souvenir sombreros and toy donkeys in straw hats. We thought they were typically Spanish. We couldn't resist.'

Yet the home-coming was not the happy occasion Christine dreamed of.

'I opened the front door and instead of seeming pleased to see me, Dad was looking very serious. "You'd better phone Kevin's mum." he said.'

Mystified, Christine dialled the familiar number. 'I'm so sorry, Christine,' said Kevin's mum in an odd, strangled voice, 'but Kevin's dead.'

One night while Christine was away, Kevin had been riding home on his motorbike when a car pulled out in front of him, and he crashed straight into it. He was taken to hospital, but his injuries were so severe, nothing could be done to save him. He died shortly afterwards. Christine, still in Spain, completely unaware of the tragedy, didn't even get the chance to say goodbye.

'I was devastated,' said Christine. 'For the next six months, I think, I went a little mad. I had to go to work as usual, but I was like a zombie. I couldn't eat, couldn't sleep, couldn't imagine a life without Kevin.'

Distraught, she began visiting spiritualist churches, desperate for a message from her fiancé but the mediums always passed her by. If Kevin really was up there looking down on her, why did he have nothing to say? Christine wondered, bitterly.

Kevin's best friend Tony, also deeply distressed, took to dropping in and – for a time – the two found comfort in each other. A couple of years later, confusing shared grief with love, they even married, but almost immediately realised their mistake. They parted amicably within 12 months but remained lifelong friends.

'And so I went back to the churches,' said Christine, 'but I was becoming more and more discouraged. I never got a message from Kevin and I didn't know what to do. Then, one day, someone told me about this Doris Stokes and her book. I didn't see how it could help, but out of curiosity I bought a copy. To my surprise, I couldn't put it down. I raced through it in about a day. I found it enormously comforting and I can honestly say it changed my life.

'From that moment on, the desperation melted away. I knew Kevin was ok. Instead of frantically going from church to church, I began learning everything I could about spiritual things. Gradually, the course of my whole future changed. I lost interest in window-dressing and began studying spiritual subjects, eventually making my career in that field. Something that would never have occurred to me before reading Voices.'

While Christine was coming to terms with her loss, over in Belgrave Square, at the SAGB, Tom Johanson also noticed something unusual was stirring. Doris' visits were becoming more and more popular and requests for her return more frequent.

'One day she suggested we do a two-part workshop but compressed into one day, to save time,' said Tom. 'The first part we could hold in the afternoon, Doris said, and the second part, the same evening. That seemed fine to me, but the morning of the workshop I had the fright of my life.

'When I arrived in Belgrave Square I found a queue of people from the SAGB front door stretching right along to the other end of the street. Nobody could get into the other offices, round about, for the crowds. People had been queuing since the night before and, in the end, the police were called.

'It was totally unexpected. Our room only held 180, and you can't get a quart in a pint pot. People kept coming up to me and saying 'I've been here since eight last night,' and I'd say, 'I know. I'm sorry but I still only have 180 seats. If you want, you can come in and sit on the stairs. So we had all these people sitting in the hall and up the stairs and we opened all the doors so even if they couldn't see her, they could hear what Doris was saying. We did our best but we were completely taken by surprise and it was chaos. After that, we had to introduce ticket-only events to keep things under control.'

Meanwhile, down at the mail sorting office for the Fulham area, postal workers were taken aback by a deluge of letters suddenly arriving for the same unassuming address in Sir Oswald Stoll Mansions, just off the high street. Mail by the sackful began to pour into Doris' tiny flat. In fact, we began to feel sorry for the poor postman who had to haul the heavy bags up to the second floor. There were so many letters that the name Doris Stokes became well-known to the sorting office. So much so that one day an envelope addressed simply to: 'Doris Stokes, Somewhere in London,' was correctly delivered.

Doris would sit for hours, reading all the letters and frequently was so moved by the plight of the writer, she'd rush to the phone and call them to offer comfort. Her phone bill must have been enormous.

'No-one escapes tragedy in this life,' she explained one day when I arrived to find her toiling over yet another sackful of mail, discarded envelopes piling up all over the carpet, 'and when it happens, they're glad of someone like me. Listen to what's happened to this poor soul...' and she'd read an extract of some heart-rending story.

The fact that a letter got through, despite having no address, seemed to Doris to be a sign that she was meant to respond. So she took a particular interest in this one. Inside were just a few brief lines. 'Doris I've been terribly bereaved. Please, please phone me, Vivienne.'

Doris – always impulsive – went straight to the phone and called the number. It turned out to be the Two Eyes restaurant in Shirley, Southampton, run by the parents of young advertising agency boss, Craig Hamilton-Parker. Craig remembers the day well.

'Someone's asking for Vivienne!' said the waitress who answered the phone.

'Vivienne's my sister,' explained Craig. 'She'd married this New Zealand guy called Wayne but then, soon after the wedding, there was terrible news. Wayne was diagnosed with cancer and was given only six months to live. It wasn't long before poor Vivienne was a young widow. Obviously, she was devastated. Anyway, around this time Voices in my Ear came out and Vivienne read it and became desperate to speak to Doris. So she wrote that letter, not even knowing where to send it. Quite honestly, we didn't expect it would ever get to Doris, let alone that Doris would answer.'

But, incredibly, here was Doris on the line. Vivienne was found and brought to the phone. 'Hello luvvie,' said Doris, 'I've got someone called Wayne here.'

'Well that did it,' recalled Craig. 'Vivienne hadn't mentioned her husband or his name or the circumstances in her letter. There was no way Doris could have known. Viv burst into tears but just talking on the phone helped her tremendously. Doris arranged for her to visit the Stokes' flat and have a proper sitting and it comforted her very much. In fact, from that moment on, it transformed her life. She was able to be happy again.'

What's more, Craig's father, Don, who didn't believe in such nonsense but was keen to do anything to ease his daughter's pain, went with her.

'And he got the shock of his life,' said Craig. 'Doris had a message for him too, from my grandmother, his wife's mother. She got her name, Mary, the names of family members including my brother Ian and his wife Jackie, and then she told him that Mary said he had two businesses and he was selling one to help fund the other.' Don was shocked because this was true but it was a secret. He'd told no one. He had a newsagent's shop as well as the restaurant, and recently he'd made the decision to sell the newsagent's to invest more in Two Eye's.

'What's more,' Doris went on, 'Mary says that in a few years' time, the other business is going to go and – when it does – it will go down like a pack of cards.' And she was right. Sometime later, that's exactly what happened.'

But that wasn't the end of the family association with Doris. Sometime later, Vivienne returned to Sir Oswald Stoll Mansions for a second visit. 'There were various troubles going on and she wanted to ask Doris for advice,' said Craig, 'and for some reason, this time she asked me to go with her.'

At that point, Craig was a successful advertising man with his own agency employing 14 staff and with prestigious accounts including the Midland Bank and Zurich Life. He was young, drove a smart Triumph Stag to work, and appeared to be heading for the top; yet, he wasn't a happy man. His marriage had disintegrated and he was bringing up his baby daughter alone – at a time when single dads were rare.

'Doris had made such a difference to Vivienne, I was interested to see her for myself,' said Craig. 'So we went over to her flat in Fulham. After greeting Vivienne, she turned to me and said: 'You're going to be a medium one day.'

Craig was an open-minded type but he had no plans in that direction. 'No, I don't think I want to do that,' he told Doris, but she was adamant. 'Yes, you're going to elevate your life,' she insisted.

'Then, to my surprise, she started giving me business advice,' Craig recalled, 'though I doubt if she knew anything about the advertising world. She said I ought to be trying for the BA account – which was true – and also that I would be working with a company called Circle or that had Circle in its name or logo. Years later, I formed a close internet partnership with a company called The Circle. She also said that I was going to meet a lady called Jane – Jane Wallis – and that we'd end up getting married. As I was recently divorced, I had no intention of re-marrying but – again – Doris was adamant. 'And you'll meet her on the 6th March,' she added. I thought this was all highly unlikely but as it was in the future you couldn't say whether she was right or wrong, so I let it ride. After a while, our sitting ended and Vivienne and I were heading for the door; just as we were leaving, Doris gave a little gasp and said: 'Oh no... and the baby's gone missing hasn't it?'

This was quite staggering. Through a complicated mix-up over visiting arrangements, some days before, Craig's nanny had mistakenly handed the baby to another family member, not realising Craig no longer had an address for them. Now Craig didn't know where his daughter was, or when she'd be back, and he had no means of making contact.

'I was very worried,' said Craig, 'but Doris told me the baby was fine and where to find her. There's no way she could have known, and it was such an unusual occurrence. It was not the sort of thing you could have guessed about a stranger. But, sure enough, my daughter was missing and we found her just where Doris had told me.'

Craig was impressed. So impressed that, even though he had no ambitions to become a medium, he joined a local development group just to see what would happen.

'I joined the circle of Peter Close, a well-known medium in Hammersmith who was also a policeman,' said Craig. 'He told me that another medium had predicted to me that this would happen. He was right of course. It was Doris.'

To Craig's surprise, as the months passed, he discovered he did seem to have an aptitude for psychic work.

Gradually, his confidence increased, and after a while, he found himself accepting invitations to demonstrate his work at spiritualist meetings. It was still very much a spare time activity though. Craig's real job, he always thought, was that of an advertising executive.

'Then one day, a few years later, I was working at the Spiritualist Church in Eastleigh, near Southampton,' said Craig. 'My first message of the night was for a lady in blue, from someone calling herself Ethel Wallis and her granddaughter, said Ethel was called Jane. A lady in blue right at the back of the hall confirmed this was true. She was called Jane, and her late grandmother was Ethel Wallis. I gave Jane some more information from her grandmother, who also told me I should ask Jane for a reading for myself as she was a medium too!

'Afterwards, when the event was over, Jane stayed behind to chat.'

Close up, Craig could see she was very attractive with soft, blonde hair and beautiful eyes. There was an immediate rapport between them, and they arranged to meet again. That's when Craig realised the date. It was March 6th and his new friend was called Jane, Jane Willis.

'Ok, so Doris got her Willis and Wallis a little mixed up,' said Craig, 'but that's understandable considering both names were in the family.'

Doris sadly passed away not long after this but by a strange coincidence, Jane had met the Rev Terry Carter who was a friend of Doris and also Doris' husband John. As romance with Craig blossomed, Rev Carter and John Stokes both became friends of the couple. 'Eventually, Jane and I got married on April 1st 1988,' said Craig, 'and Jane asked John to give her away at our wedding. So, just a few years after Doris predicted our marriage, I looked down the aisle to see Doris' husband John walking my bride to the altar.'

Not long afterwards, Craig found himself more and more disillusioned with the advertising business. Though he was earning good money and enjoying the trappings of success, he decided to swap it all for the uncertain life of full-time medium.

'With Jane's whole-hearted support,' said Craig. 'These days we work together. It's strange, Doris often said she didn't do predictions. She was not a fortune-teller. Yet she made a whole series of predictions for me and they all came true – even though some came about, years later. Incredible.

'And to think, if it hadn't been for Viv reading that book – it's quite possible that none of this would have happened.'

CHAPTER 6

Doris was excited. She was off on her travels again. America this time. Since the first book had come out, we'd been asked to write several sequels and Doris had made a number of overseas trips. She'd noticed though, as she moved through various airports and negotiated the baggage carousels at the other end, that the Stokes' family suitcases – old, battered and possibly pre-war – looked decidedly shabby amongst the sleek, glamorous pieces of luggage circulating lazily before the assembled passengers.

'I'm going to get some new cases!' she whispered to me, hand over the mouthpiece of the phone as I arrived. 'Oh yes is that Harrods?' she said back into the receiver.

Harrods? I must have raised my eyebrows in surprise.

'They sell everything you know!' she whispered. 'Oh yes. Hello luv. Do you do suitcases? ... Oh good. I'd like to buy some new ones ... What sort? ...' Doris frowned. She had no idea and had never set foot in Harrods' luggage department. She had little conception of the variety, brands, designer or non-designer, or sheer number of options available. Or the prices that a simple suitcase could command. 'All matching,' she said at last. 'Yes I'd like a set of suitcases, all matching.'

Goodness knows what they sent her, and how much it cost, but Doris put the phone down quite happy. No longer would she and John be shamed in posh hotels by inferior luggage.

By now the books were selling well and, for the first time in her life, Doris realised she didn't have to scrimp and save. Doris wasn't wealthy – as any author knows, having a book published doesn't usually make you a millionaire –

but having been on a tight budget all her life, she felt comfortable now. And her tastes were very simple.

Apart from her 'Rent-a-tent' frocks as she called them – discreet, floor length dresses she bought to wear on stage – a weekly hair-do and an endless supply of cigarettes, Doris had very few needs and there was little to spend her money on.

When we were working on the books, her favourite lunch, which she put together herself, was a tinned salmon sandwich mashed with a hearty splash of a vinegar and a good shake from the pepper pot. As for alcohol, I don't think she was against it, but I can't recall ever seeing her drink anything stronger than tea.

Breakfast was always porridge. Doris' best friend, Nancy, who lived on the floor above and visited most days, recalled: 'Breakfast was always porridge and tears. That's what I called it anyway. When I went round at breakfast time there'd be carrier bags of mail all over the kitchen floor and Doris was opening letters as she ate her porridge and crying her eyes out. 'Look at this one Nancy,' she'd say, showing me some heart-wrenching note. 'Isn't it dreadful?'

And she seldom went out – unless she had to make a public appearance somewhere. Doris rarely left her flat, not even to buy groceries.

It was odd. The first time I saw her, she'd been walking back from the high street with John, and at that point she was also regularly taking herself up the road to her development class without a qualm. Yet, as the years passed, those trips became less and less frequent until I began to realise they'd stopped altogether. Strange that she could stand up on a stage in front of thousands of people without a tremor, or chat happily to an unknown presenter in a TV studio, yet moving out of her own front door and walking down the street had become an unwelcome challenge.

She told me once that as a nurse, years before, she'd been attacked and kicked in the throat by a mental patient, sustaining serious injuries and surgery in hospital. Though she recovered physically, the mental scars remained. She tried to go back to work but found her nerve had gone. She began to suffer what we'd probably call panic attacks these days. At times, overwhelmed by fear, she froze at the sight of an oncoming patient even though they meant her no harm. Hiding away at home and resting for months on end made no difference. In the end, Doris realised she'd never be able to go back to her old job.

So, basically, she retired. Then, as she felt stronger, she concentrated on doing a few gentle 'sittings' at home and low-key demonstrations at the local spiritualist churches. This approach must have worked because her nerves seemed to settle, and by the time she arrived in London, she thought she'd got over it. At first she went out and about with John, travelling on public transport to various churches in the area and making new friends.

Yet, ironically, it seemed that as her success grew, so the panic attacks returned. She developed what was possibly a type of agoraphobia. It didn't seem significant at the time; after all, she worked so hard she was understandably tired between engagements and, of course, she wasn't getting any younger. Surely it wasn't surprising if she didn't feel like dashing out on errands afterwards? So it never occurred to me to ask her about it.

Yet, increasingly, unless she had to venture out for professional reasons, she wasn't comfortable leaving home. Could it be that as her fame grew, and she was recognised and approached by strangers in the street, it brought back that old sense of vulnerability? Who knows?

'It was such a contradiction,' said Tony Ortzen who'd noticed it too. 'Doris could stand on stage in front of thousands of people yet she couldn't walk down the street to the supermarket.'

She also found it difficult to eat in front of others. Throat surgery had left her with a fear of choking and at the fancy dinners to which she was occasionally invited she'd pick at the rich dishes in front of her, scarcely swallowing a thing.

Yet, Doris was in no way isolated. She may not have wanted to go out, but people came to her. The flat was small but it was open-house and visitors were constantly popping in and out and finding a warm welcome at any time. John fetched the day to day provisions from Doris' shopping lists, and they found a hairdresser who'd do home visits (an essential, as Doris fought a regular battle with her thick, springy hair); for everything else, Doris had her trusty telephone, landline of course. She loved a chat and, between visitors, she was always on the phone to one friend or other, or calling some grief-stricken person who'd sent a particularly devastating letter. Her phone bill was frightening.

'Doris, your phone bill is astronomical. You'll have to do something about it,' scolded her accountant a few years later when she needed help to sort out her finances. 'You'll have to cut down.'

'I know it's bad,' she said to me afterwards, 'but he doesn't understand. I can't cut down. Some of those calls are urgent.'

Yet, shopping could be a problem. In those days – before mobiles, laptops and the internet – home deliveries seemed like a relic from the Victorian age. With the exception of the milkman, the postman, and possibly the paper boy, home deliveries had almost disappeared. Clothes, plants, and minor items could be bought through-mail order catalogues, but for most other things, you *had* to visit a store, even if just to place an order.

Which was tricky for Doris. She didn't need much, but when she did, this was a dilemma. Yet, suddenly, with more money flowing in, there was a solution. We'd all heard of Harrods, the swanky Knightsbridge store famous for selling everything. It was said you could even order a real, live elephant from Harrods. Doris didn't need an elephant, of course, but more precious to her was Harrods' reliable reputation and delivery service.

So when she called Harrods for suitcases, she wasn't being grand – it was the only place she could think of to shop for everything, without leaving home.

Doris' other lifeline was her newspaper. Every day she read her Sun or Mirror from cover to cover. As usual, a particularly sad story would move her to tears, particularly if it involved children. This had always been the case, but now she realised, things had changed. Now she was earning more money, she could help.

'Look at this, isn't it dreadful? Poor little lad,' she said one day when I arrived. She held out the paper and showed me a report about a small boy, who was deaf, who'd had his expensive, state-of-the-art hearing-aid smashed by bullies. His mother couldn't afford to replace it.

Doris was incensed at the callousness of the hard-hearted lads who'd do such a thing. Immediately, she was on the phone to the paper, asking the reporter to speak to the mum and arrange for Doris to buy the boy a new hearing-aid.

Not long after this, another depressing report caught her eye. A baby at Basildon hospital in Essex had died and it was said that if only the hospital had more foetal heart monitors, perhaps the child could have been saved. Doris, who'd lost a baby herself, found this heart-breaking.

Without the faintest idea how much such equipment cost, she was soon dialling directory enquiries for the number of the hospital so she could buy them a foetal heart monitor. If it saved babies' lives, it was money well spent she reckoned.

Around this time, she also received a letter from a couple called Jim and Jo McDonald. They'd almost lost a baby themselves they explained, from an apparently new and baffling syndrome known as cot death. Throughout the '70s and '80s the press was full of distressing stories of seemingly healthy babies being put to bed apparently fit and well, only to be found dead in their cots next morning. Sudden Infant Death Syndrome, as the medical world called it, was a tragic and baffling phenomenon and during those years thousands of babies died. The McDonalds decided to start a charity – the Cot Death Research Appeal – to raise money for research into the syndrome and also for counselling for bereaved parents.

'We were looking for a president for the charity,' Jo recalled, 'and we thought Doris would be perfect. So we wrote to her.' They expected it would take weeks to receive a reply – if they got a reply at all – but to their surprise, Doris rang them immediately.

'She said she'd be honoured to help,' said Jo. 'We expected her time would be limited as we knew she was very much in demand, but whenever we asked her to speak to bereaved parents she never said 'no'. 'She must have comforted hundreds of parents – right up until the time she went into hospital with her last illness – and she also gave substantial donations towards vital research.'

Then there was special equipment she bought for a school for the blind, the minibus to take disabled children out on treats, and goodness knows how many other worthy causes that caught her eye.

Even on visits to churches, Doris ran into people who needed more than spiritual comfort.

'People were always coming up to her and saying 'Can you give me £50? I'm desperate' or 'I really need a holiday but I can't afford it,' said Ray Robinson, son of old friend Derek, who has since taken over from his late father as President of Wimbledon Church, 'and Doris would never turn them away.'

Even the headquarters of the SAGB benefited from Doris' generosity. 'Our restaurant was looking shabby and we needed new chairs, 'recalled Tom Johannsson, 'but as a registered charity, funds were limited. When Doris got to hear about it she bought us 12 new tables with 48 beautiful new chairs to match.'

Doris, who came from a very poor background and had struggled most of her life, never forgot what it was like to be in need. 'My dad always used to tell me: 'Cast your bread upon the waters girl, and it'll come back buttered'.' she was fond of recalling – and she certainly seemed to be taking his advice. No wonder then that, when she finally passed away, it was reported she left an estate of just £15,000.

The media was aghast. There was talk of secret Swiss bank accounts or hidden hoards but no other money was ever found. When her adopted son Terry passed away a few years later, it was said there wasn't even enough cash left to bury him, which would have distressed Doris greatly.

I'm not really surprised. I doubt Doris was anywhere near as wealthy as the press guess-timated. She wasn't motivated by money and probably made no attempt to keep track of her finances. Plus, of course, she gave away thousands.

That's not to say Doris was a saint. As she was the first to admit. When she was tired or worried, she could be irritable with the people closest to her; but for the bereaved, or those in genuine need, she had endless compassion.

'I remember once I was in church to conduct a funeral,' said Ray Robinson, 'and suddenly I heard this whispering. It was the undertaker trying to attract my attention. 'I met that Doris Stokes once,' he wanted to tell me. He said he'd recently lost his son and wanted a sitting with Doris but she was well known by this time, extremely busy, and you couldn't get a sitting for love nor money. Anyway, he found out where she lived in Sir Oswald Stoll Mansions, went over there late one night and knocked on the door. Most people would have turned him away but Doris welcomed him in, gave him a cup of tea and did a sitting for him. He found it very comforting. As it happened, at that point Doris had recently been criticised quite harshly in the press so I suggested he contact the papers and tell his story. The man agreed the comments were unfair but he wouldn't approach the paper. He didn't want to draw attention to himself.'

Doris' soft heart extended to animals as well as people. Picking up the Daily Mirror one morning, she found herself looking into the mournful eyes of a little Jack Russell-Dachshund-cross puppy that was languishing, unloved in a rescue centre. Tiny 'Boots' the story explained, had been abandoned twice already and he was still only 10 weeks old. Doris was so moved by the plight of the little fellow she immediately rang the rescue centre to offer him a home. Which is how the lively bundle of black and tan fur became the newest addition to the Stokes household.

'Isn't he gorgeous!' said Doris when I came round to see him. She smiled fondly as the cheeky pup dashed up and down the sitting room, skidding over our feet, and pausing only to chew at the hearthrug. 'He's made himself at home already. How could anyone abandon him?'

CHAPTER 7

'Are you quite sure Andre?' Jenne Casarotto, Doris' book agent, wasn't certain she'd heard correctly. 'I mean the Edinburgh Festival? The Fringe? Doris isn't exactly rock and roll is she…?'

A new generation of young, stand-up comedians were just beginning to hone their skills at the increasingly famous event. Alternative comedy they called it, and the punkish performers were the hottest acts in town. Edinburgh's streets heaved with students, the hip, and the fashionable under-thirties, and they were pouring into the theatres to see these new-wave stars-to-be. What on earth, Jenne wondered, could have made her old friend Andre Ptaszynski imagine an OAP like Doris was right for Scotland's coolest event?

'I thought he was mad,' said Jenne, now distinguished head of international Film, TV and Theatre agency, Casarotto, Ramsay & Associates. 'It was crazy. Doris was this cosy, grandma sort of lady. I couldn't see how she would fit in somewhere like the Fringe.'

But Andre persisted. To be honest, by the sound of it, even he thought it was a bit of a gamble.

'At the time,' recalled Andre, 'I was just starting out and trying to set up my own production company. Basically, I was looking for some sort of project, a theatre project, to earn a little bit of money to get going.'

Back then, young Andre couldn't have guessed just how brilliantly he'd succeed. These days he's a renowned executive producer, having worked with Andrew Lloyd Webber as Chief executive of Lloyd Webber's Really Useful Group, as well as producing a host of award-winning TV series and theatre shows, including Matilda the Musical, and Groundhog Day.

But at the dawn of the '80s and not long out of university, Andre needed to get his fledgling company off the ground.

'I had a friend called Martin Bergman who'd spent a lot of time in Australia, and one day he phoned to tell me about this woman he'd seen on TV over there. She was called Doris Stokes, he said, and they were lapping her up in Australia. Why didn't I look into doing something with her?'

Andre was unsure. 'I was a bit uneasy about working with a medium,' he said, 'but when I realised Jenne was her agent I was reassured. Jenne was a very distinguished agent, and I knew she wouldn't take on just anyone.'

So Andre met Doris and John at the Stokes' flat.

'Doris was a very warm, empathetic lady with these milky blue eyes that could suddenly become very intense,' said Andre. 'I didn't want a sitting. I didn't think that would be professional, but Doris tried. 'Do you have someone in your family called Maria?' she asked. So I said, 'Doris, with a surname like Ptaszynski, of course there's someone in my family called Maria! How could there not be?' So, she didn't go any further. But I have to admit, though I didn't tell Doris, my grandmother's name was Maria.'

Despite his rejection of a sitting, Doris wasn't offended, and she agreed to give the Festival a try.

'I was also putting on some comedians from New York at the Festival,' said Andre. 'The comedians sold out. Doris didn't sell out; she half sold out.'

But the results were encouraging enough for Andre to continue. He booked some theatres in provincial towns, and even tried a brief foray to Baltimore in the USA, but nothing seemed to work as well as he'd hoped.

'I thought I'd give it one last go,' he explained. 'We booked St Pancras Town Hall in London. It was cheap as chips, and we didn't bother with a lot of advertising. Just a couple of small ads in the local papers. On the night, I picked Doris up from Fulham, drove her across to St Pancras and – as we pulled up outside the Town Hall – we saw 1,000 people queuing to get in.'

Andre was astonished. By sheer chance, he seemed to have found the right formula. 'Town Halls, lecture halls, smaller venues, and adverts in the local papers. We'd found our audience.'

Little by little, Doris' life was changing. Time now had to be set aside to work on the books, and her theatre appearances were on the increase.

In fact, the live shows had started in a small way, long before she met Andre, while she was waiting for the first book to appear, as Ray Robinson of Wimbledon church recalled.

'Around this time, Gordon Higginson (still President of the SNU and based at Stansted Hall) and my Dad were worried that people weren't coming to the spiritualist churches like they had in the past,' said Ray. 'The congregations were dwindling. Gordon thought the answer was to go back to spiritualism's roots, to take it out of the churches and back into the community. 'If the people won't come to the church,' said Gordon, 'the church must go to the people.'

'So Gordon, Dad, Doris and another medium friend, Jessie Nathan, came up with a plan. They decided they'd go out into halls and theatres around the country giving live demonstrations, to show people what spiritualism was all about. My dad wasn't a medium himself, but he was a brilliant organiser; so he volunteered to book the venues, and arrange the advertising and the tickets, while the three mediums would appear on stage. They called the group Life After Death Promotions.'

Derek quickly got to work and, soon, the three mediums were on the road.

'At first, when Doris – a complete unknown – appeared, we'd get an audience of about 30 people,' said Ray, 'but gradually the numbers increased until soon she was filling a 1,300 seater hall on her own.'

And as Doris' fame grew and word of her popular books spread, the halls got bigger and bigger, the media became interested, and requests to appear overseas rolled in.

'It got to the stage,' said Andre, 'that we could book the City Hall, Sheffield, which was a 2,000 seater and Doris filled it. I saw her do some extraordinary things. One that stands out was that night in Sheffield.

'At one point Doris was looking for someone with the initial E and eventually gestured to row L which she wouldn't have been able to see clearly from the stage. She got some messages for this woman who was called Elaine. Then she said, 'And that woman sitting in the row behind you – that's your sister Maureen isn't it?'

And it was. Then Doris' arm swung round, and she pointed past them, right out to the very back of the theatre – literally the back row – row ZZ it must have been, which she wouldn't have been able to see at all and she said to someone sitting there: 'I bet you're feeling stupid now aren't you? You're Elaine and Maureen's brother aren't you? And you weren't going to come. You said it was a load of rubbish, didn't you?'

'And the man admitted he actually was their brother and that's what he'd said. He didn't believe in mediums, but he agreed to drop his sisters off at the City Hall and intended to go to the pub and have a pint before picking them up afterwards. Yet, for some reason, when he got to the pub he didn't want to stay. So he turned around, went back to the theatre and found there was just one ticket left – right at the back of the house. So, he bought it. That's why he wasn't sitting with his sisters. They didn't even know he was there.'

Andre was so amazed by this story, he could hardly believe it was true. So, after the show, he went to the box office to check.

'They told me it was quite right. That seat was the last one left in the house and the young man had bought it at 7.27 pm that night – three minutes before the show was to start.'

Doris appeared quite unfazed. The incident didn't seem odd to her. 'I don't think for a minute that she doubted her voices,' concluded Andre.

As the months went on, and we continued to work on her books, it gradually dawned on us that Doris was becoming a household name. This was a turn of events we'd never foreseen. As far as we knew, there'd never been a celebrity medium before (according to Wikipedia Doris was the first), so there was no previous example to show us what might happen next or the possibilities that could open up – both good and bad – or how to handle them.

We'd never seen any other medium's autobiographies on the bookstalls until then, or heard of mediums appearing in large theatres or on TV and radio the way Doris did. At that time, becoming a medium would never have been thought of as a route to fame and fortune.

Such an idea had never entered Doris' head. She didn't have a game plan. She'd been doing her sittings and demonstrating at Spiritualist churches for decades and reached the age of 60 more or less broke, and virtually unknown. If fame and fortune had been her goal, she'd surely have given up years before, to try something else.

So she simply carried on, the only way she knew. She moved forward, one day at a time, accepting every request she could fit into her calendar – just like she'd always done. There was no overall scheme and Doris remained quite unchanged. She simply went where she seemed to be needed – the way she always did.

Then one winter afternoon, I called at the flat to work on the latest volume of memoirs and found an unfamiliar figure standing on the orange hearth-rug.

'Come and meet Laurie,' called Doris from her usual armchair. 'He's my new manager.'

Manager? Since when had Doris had a manager? I looked at him a little suspiciously. Laurie O'Leary had a friendly smile, light brown hair, and was smartly dressed in a navy blue blazer and shiny black shoes.

'Nice to meet you,' said Laurie, warmly shaking my hand.

He seemed pleasant enough but I was confused. Where had he come from all of a sudden? Doris hadn't mentioned needing a manager before. As I heard more about this Laurie, I became even more confused. Laurie's background was show business – particularly the music business. He'd run London's famous Speakeasy Club – home of the in-est of the in-crowd. He had rubbed shoulders with the Beatles, the Rolling Stones, and The Who, and said he'd managed and worked with some of the biggest names of the era: Marvin Gay, Martha Reeves and the Vandellas, Otis Redding, and more. Very impressive, but I couldn't see how this fitted in with Doris in any way.

Tony Ortzen felt the same, though for slightly different reasons. 'I was polite and friendly,' said Tony, 'but I was wary at first. I'd heard Laurie was a friend of the Kray Twins which didn't seem a good connection.'

It turned out that Laurie was a genuine East Ender who'd grown up around the corner from the notorious Kray home in Vallance Road, Bethnal Green. His mum knew their mum and, as children, the boys played together; they ran in and out of each other's houses and attended the same school. As they grew up, Laurie was drawn into football while the Krays preferred boxing and as the twins moved on into villainy, Laurie insisted their paths diverge further. Laurie remained on friendly terms with the family but stayed out of Ronnie and Reggie's terrifying gang. He always maintained that he refused, point blank, to do anything criminal.

The twins, who had vicious tempers, 'they were good friends but dangerous enemies,' as Laurie explained later, apparently accepted this. They remained lifelong mates and Laurie visited Ronnie regularly in prison until his death. In fact, later, he even took Doris to Broadmoor to meet him.

Yet until then, it had never entered Doris' head to look for a manager. So, how had Laurie ended up in front of the coal-effect electric fire that chilly afternoon?

As so often with Doris' affairs, it was all down to chance it seemed. Some months earlier, a friend of Laurie's wife, Iris, had bought two tickets to a demonstration Doris was giving in Walthamstow. Iris had agreed to accompany her friend but, at the last minute, got an attack of nerves.

'I thought she was a fortune-teller,' Iris explained anxiously to Laurie that evening, 'but apparently, she talks to the dead, and I don't want to talk to the dead. I really don't want to go. Would you take Maureen instead, Laurie? She'll be so upset if I let her down.'

Laurie said later that he'd never heard of this Doris Stokes, but he was devoted to Iris, and curious to see what the show was all about, so he agreed to keep Maureen company.

'When I arrived at Walthamstow, there were so many people queuing outside I thought I must be in the wrong place,' he said, 'but I checked, and this was the Doris Stokes event. I was impressed. I'd never heard of her, but she seemed to attract a big crowd.'

Once he got inside the hall though, he was disappointed with the sight that greeted the audience. 'There was a very stark, bare stage,' said Laurie, 'with a table rather like a kitchen table in the centre, with two chairs – one on each side – and a little posy of flowers on the top. And that was it.'

To Laurie's professional eye, accustomed to lavish, rock concert staging, it was underwhelming to say the least. 'I thought, Oh God, are we going to be singing hymns? It was a bit like the local Methodist church and I didn't feel right at all.'

Yet, as the evening wore on, Laurie found himself drawn in.

'Doris had such presence; she held my attention all evening,' he said. But he remained ambivalent about the 'entertainment'. All those people picked out from the audience to receive supposed messages from departed love ones – some moving, some funny. It didn't seem possible. It had to be an elaborate fake.

'Those people who get the messages – they're obviously all plants,' he said to Maureen on the way home. 'Got to be. I mean if what she's doing was true, it would be marvellous. But, if not, then she's a very wicked woman and I'd like to expose her.'

'But suppose she's genuine?' asked Maureen.

Laurie shrugged, thinking it highly unlikely. 'Well if she's genuine, I'd like to manage her.'

It was just a throwaway remark, particularly as – at that point – Laurie had taken a break from management and for 'relaxation' was running a pub instead. He wasn't looking for any more clients. Yet Maureen sensed his interest was real, so when they got back, she lent him a copy of one of Doris' books.

'I read it,' said Laurie, 'and I was even more intrigued. I thought, surely she can't write a book like this if it's all lies?'

As it happened, the Krays' beloved mother Violet had passed away a year or so before. They might have been brutal gangsters but those tough, ruthless twins genuinely worshipped their mum and Laurie thought Doris' book might comfort Ronnie, so he posted him a copy in Broadmoor.

'Ronnie not only read it, he liked it so much he wrote back and asked if he could meet this Doris Stokes,' said Laurie. 'So I contacted the tour promotors who'd arranged the Walthamstow show and explained the situation. I asked if Doris would agree to speak to me.'

To everyone's surprise, Doris agreed. What they didn't realise then was that Doris agreed to almost everything. I rarely heard her refuse a request if it was in her power to accept.

'Doris wasn't put off by Ronnie's past,' said Laurie. 'She always said it's what people make of their lives now that counts, and if a man like Ronnie was becoming interested in spiritual things, that was a good sign.'

As it turned out, Ronnie was on his gentlemanly best behaviour when Doris arrived at Broadmoor and she was charmed by him. Apparently, he offered her a smoked salmon sandwich and a pork pie by way of light refreshment – though it wasn't clear where or how he might have obtained these delicacies. Fortunately, Doris politely declined and settled instead for a cup of tea. By all accounts, they had an enjoyable afternoon and Doris reckoned she picked up Ronnie's mum and passed on some messages from mother to son.

She came away impressed. 'Ronnie was so polite!' she said afterwards. 'And his cell! He had big armchairs with antimacassars, and the prison warders served us tea.' I think she believed the former villain had finally changed his ways and seen the light.

The more he saw of Doris, the more intrigued Laurie became, and he asked if he could accompany her on some of her theatre visits, at his own expense. Privately, he'd made up his mind to catch her out if she was a fake. How on earth was she pulling this off, he wondered.

'If it was a con, I wanted to know how she was doing it,' said Laurie. He thought he was being discreet in his investigations, 'But backstage one night, she suddenly said: 'You're checking up on me aren't you Laurie? D'you want to follow me to the loo?"'

'Of course not,' Laurie protested. 'Well, that's what one reporter did,' she said. 'He actually came with me to the loo and stood there watching to see if I flushing away hidden notes.'

After watching her closely through several events, Laurie realised it would have been impossible for Doris to memorise all the correct facts and names she mentioned night after night – names and facts that changed every night too. 'Also, I mingled with the crowds as they left the theatres and listened to the comments the people were making as they went home,' said Laurie. 'They seemed happy. Elated, some of them. I realised Doris was very good for them. They felt much better for seeing her.'

In the end, he was so impressed, he offered to be Doris' manager.

'Why do I need a manager?' asked Doris. 'Isn't that a bit grand?'

'You can't possibly cope with all this,' Laurie pointed out; which was true. The way Doris' fame was increasing, with requests for appearances snowballing, she and John couldn't hope to deal with organising the details and sorting out her diary. 'But if you don't like the word 'manager', you could say I was your promoter,' Laurie added. 'And you don't need to pay me. I'll make my money from the promotions.'

So, by pure chance, Doris acquired a 'free' manager and it's said, throughout their time together, they didn't even have a written contract.

Laurie quickly became indispensable. He organised theatre bookings, travel arrangements, overnight stays, and just about everything else. Always cheerful and calm, nothing appeared to be too much trouble. Laurie was even known to pick up a cauliflower on his way over for the Stokes' tea, if John had forgotten to buy one at the greengrocers.

Doris was a bit bemused but tremendously thrilled when Laurie arranged a fancy car to chauffeur her to her appearances in style. She was a star, he insisted, and it was important she arrived as rested and refreshed as possible. No more waiting for trains on draughty station platforms. Soon, she was appearing at the nation's most prestigious theatres including London's Barbican and the Palladium.

'She must have appeared at the Palladium eight times,' recalled Tony Ortzen, 'and I chaired for her at those shows.'

The extraordinary thing was that Doris' theatre shows were very like the demonstrations she used to give at the spiritualist churches in the old days, but on a grander scale and without any preliminary prayers or hymn singing. She had no script, act, or other performers. There were no props other than a chair, table, and some flowers to make the place look more attractive. She required only a microphone and a presenter to step out on the stage first, and introduce her to the audience.

Tony Ortzen performed this role after work in the Psychic News office, whenever he could – which usually meant Doris' appearances in places close to home such as London and Brighton.

Looking back now, Tony marvels at the way Doris – with no theatrical training, no act and very little idea of what she was going to say – could step out in front of huge audiences and keep them entertained for hours.

'My part was very small,' said Tony. 'I just had to go out on stage and say to the audience something along the lines of: 'Ladies and Gentleman would you please welcome Doris Stokes, the lady with voices in her ear....' But even though I had so little to do, it could be unnerving. I remember walking out on the stage at the Palladium, and it's terrifying. You're on your own, and you look up and see thousands and thousands of people and row upon row of faces, going higher and higher, and I'd feel a slight tremor in my legs, and my voice would shake. But then Doris would walk out from the wings with no sign of nerves at all – despite the fact that just a few minutes before, she'd been anxiously asking John for another ciggie in her dressing-room.

'She always started off by chatting to the audience to calm them and to calm herself until the 'voices' arrived. Some nights, the messages would take longer arriving than others so she'd just chat until she could hear something and she had a few jokes she'd tell.

'Some people accuse me of raising the dead,' Doris would say, 'Raise the dead luvvie? I reply. I couldn't raise the skin off a rice pudding!'

And: 'Some people say I'm a fake. Well the only thing fake about me loves, is my boob. In fact, I've had so many operations and parts removed I think they're taking me over to the spirit world bit by bit.'

And there was her medium joke. 'A man goes to a medium and says: 'Tell me, I really love cricket. Do they play cricket on the other side?' And the medium replies: 'Well I've got good news and bad news. The good news is that yes, they do play cricket on the other side.' And the man says, 'That's excellent. So what's the bad news?' 'The bad news,' says the medium, 'is you're Captain on Sunday.'

And that was basically that, until the voices arrived.

Oddly enough, many years later, I too found myself walking onto that legendary stage. I'd never imagined that one day I'd tread the boards at the Palladium, yet long after Doris passed away, a new production of the King and I, starring Elaine Paige was opening there, and the magazine sent me to talk to various members of the cast.

For some reason, to reach their dressing-room, I had to walk across the darkened stage. I have to admit, I lingered. After all, a chance like this was unlikely ever to occur again, and I couldn't resist making the most of it. There was absolutely no reason for me to walk out towards the footlights – I should have moved briskly from wing to wing across the back wall – but I couldn't help myself!

There was no one about. The curtain was up, the stage was bare and unlit, and the theatre sat in semi-darkness. There was something eerie about those tiers and tiers of empty seats – so, so many – stretching up and up, impossibly high above your head, disappearing into the shadows. No wonder ghost stories abound in old theatres. Yet, there was something magical about the place too.

I tried to imagine those endless, velvety rows full of faces. Utterly terrifying – just as Tony had said.

No wonder his legs shook. Possibly I was standing exactly where Doris had stood, all those years before, looking out into the audience. There she was, a simple, untrained pensioner who couldn't sing, couldn't dance, couldn't act, and with nothing but one weak joke about a medium with which to entertain that huge crowd, single-handed. How on earth had she done it?

CHAPTER 8

The dressing-room was warm and cosy with soft lighting and comfortable armchairs. I'd never been backstage at one of Doris' appearances before, but we were working on her latest book and I realised it was high time I saw for myself what she was doing these days.

I realise, now, that back then I was only dimly aware of the scale of the Doris phenomenon. Doris herself seemed the same as ever, and we worked – cocooned in her sitting-room over tea and tinned salmon sandwiches – just as we'd always done. From my point of view, very little had changed. Of course, Doris talked about the extraordinary things that were happening to her, but it all sounded a bit unreal. Hearing about it wasn't the same as seeing and experiencing it I realised; so here I was, notebook at hand to put that right.

Outside, it was a dark winter's night and the crowds were swirling around the theatre but, in here, Doris, John and I were encased in a snug, tranquil bubble. All the same, there was a thread of tension in the air.

Doris was sitting in the chair opposite, dressed in one of her long 'rent-a-tents' – a flowing number in muted pinks and blues – a cup of tea at her elbow. Her hair was sparkling white, her nails beautifully manicured and painted shell pink, and she'd found a lipstick to match. She looked perfect and, for all her finery, she was still the same old down-to-earth Doris. Yet, she was clearly a little nervous.

At the time, I don't think it properly occurred to me how nerve-wracking it must have been to contemplate walking out onto a stage and entertaining an audience alone, for over two hours, without even a script to fall back on. Suppose she couldn't think of anything to say? Suppose they didn't like her? Suppose they simply got bored? Surely such thoughts must have crossed her mind before every show.

Doris always said that, every night before she went to bed, she spoke to her spirit guide Ramanov for advice; so, naturally, the subject of her stage appearances came up.

Apparently, his instructions on this matter never changed: 'He always tells me to trust,' said Doris. 'He says 'Just trust, child. We've never let you down before and we'll never let you down now'.'

Which is all very well, but standing on your own, under a blazing spotlight with 2,000 expectant faces looking back at you waiting for you to wow them, would surely make the toughest stomach quake. Doris had a pretty tough stomach, but even so...

'Pass us a ciggie, John,' she said, a shade strained. And John, clearly used to this routine, dug out a cigarette, deftly lit it and handed it over. The next second Doris was puffing away gratefully, pale smoke curling into the still air.

Lung cancer? It was far too late to worry about lung cancer. Doris had faced the big C several times already and, besides, she'd been hooked since long before anyone realised cigarettes were bad for you. She wasn't going to give up now.

We were at Lewisham Theatre – Doris' local these days. Tony Ortzen, smart in bow tie and evening suit, popped his head around the door to say hello and somewhere in the auditorium, Laurie was fussing around sorting out the microphones. Doris liked to talk to the people who received messages. Some were able to walk down to microphones set up at the foot of the stage to chat to her, but when people were at the back of the theatre, it was Laurie's job, where possible, to take a mic to them.

Outside, the waiting queue stretched away into the darkness.

'It was quite incredible,' recalled theatre manager Chris Hare later. 'I'd never heard of Doris Stokes when she was first booked with us. We'd had quite a few big name acts at Lewisham but when I looked at the crowds that first night it seemed as if this Doris was bigger than anyone in the country – bar possibly Michael Jackson.

'At first, we treated her appearances like any other; we accepted phone bookings and allowed people to buy as many tickets as they wanted. But our phone lines were jammed for days, long after the seats were sold out and ticket touts started hanging around outside. In the end, we stopped all phone bookings and limited people to four or six tickets each, which had to be collected in person.'

Yet even this strategy could be worrying.

'The box office opened at ten in the morning, and when there were Doris Stokes tickets on sale, people started queuing at ten o'clock the night before. In the winter, I was concerned we'd have someone die of exposure. Once, it was so cold, we even served soup to the crowds at 6am to keep them warm.'

Just then, Chris himself – dapper, like Tony in evening-dress – looked in to say hello. 'There's another bag of letters handed in for you Doris,' he said. This apparently was a regular occurrence. Not knowing how to contact her directly, hundreds of fans left letters at the theatre.

'Thanks luv,' said Doris. 'I'll take them with me.' She took them home afterwards and read every one.

Then, Tony was back: 'Ok Doris. Time to go.'

'Come on then luv,' said Doris to me, stubbing out her cigarette. She stood up and shook the folds of her dress to dislodge any stray specks of ash or possible creases. 'You can watch from the wings.'

And then we were all hurrying through the narrow corridors to the stage. Safe in the shadows, we looked out at the dazzling floor under the lights. We could hear the buzz of the audience and feel the expectation in the air. Then Tony went out and did his introduction, Doris glided forward; there was a huge burst of applause and she was off.

She seemed to chat for quite a while and she told her familiar jokes, but there were plenty of laughs in the right places and it was clear the audience was enjoying it. Then, all at once, almost mid-sentence, Doris seemed to hear one of her voices. She immediately broke off from the story she was telling and launched into the messages.

Looking back now, the details are a blur but just one, in particular, stands out. Doris always said that even in a vast theatre, she could usually tell roughly where the recipient of a message was sitting because she could see a light dancing around beside them. Anyway, one particular woman in the audience recognised a set of names Doris mentioned and came down to the microphone at the foot of the stage. It turned out she was a mother who'd lost a young child in tragic circumstances. Tears began to roll down her face as Doris began talking to the little girl. Doris gave the name of the child, the child's age, and many other details and then she said, 'And she says you've just found her building society savings book haven't you? Just recently. And she's telling me her savings are still in it. She says she'd got £4.65...'

'Yes!' gasped the mother, laughing and crying at the same time. 'Yes, that's right. Exactly.'

In the wings, the backstage crew exchanged glances, amazed. It was such a tiny, inconsequential detail. Of no importance in itself. Yet it was the kind of thing surely no one could have guessed, overheard, or thought to make up.

Eventually, Doris was ready to move on and the mother returned to her seat. She looked ecstatic. If that woman was acting, she deserved an Oscar.

The evening ended with a standing ovation. Flowers were presented and then we all trooped back to the dressing-room. Doris, clutching her huge bouquet, was happy but drained. At this point, Lewisham's usual big name acts might have been all set for a night's clubbing but not Doris. Doris, now well over 60, wanted nothing more than to get home, change into her dressing-gown and have another cuppa before bed.

The last I saw of her, she and John were climbing into Laurie's car, with carrier bags of letters on their laps and around their feet, and her bouquet on the parcel shelf, for the short drive home.

In fact, it was a very short drive home because – these days – the Stokes family lived just up the road. They'd finally moved from Fulham out to Lee Green in south London. Once again, the upheaval had come about by chance. Doris and John had been thrilled when, in 1982, the management at Sir Oswald Stoll Mansions started upgrading the flats and the Stokes' were moved along the corridor to one of the new conversions which had a bathroom. Doris was delighted.

Their plant pots and deckchairs simply slid further up the walkway and, from the outside, their new residence looked exactly like the old one. Yet, now, the indoor coal store was gone and, for the first time in years, they were able to say goodbye to their old tin bath and enjoy a soak in a proper tub with the added luxury of a shower as well.

What's more, despite giving so much of her earnings away, Doris managed to save enough to buy a caravan in Kent so that she and John could escape to the country for a short holiday now and then.

They seemed to have everything they needed, and Doris would probably have stayed in Fulham, quite contentedly, for the rest of her life.

Yet there was to be another twist. It seemed bizarre to the Stokes' after the management had just spent so much money updating their building, but out of the blue they heard that despite the new bathrooms, their whole block was now scheduled for demolition. The other blocks in the complex were to be modernised further, and the Stokes' block would disappear altogether to make space for a communal garden. No doubt it would be lovely one day, but right now Doris and John had a choice. They could remain living on the building site for a few years until the programme was complete and they could move into one of the new flats, or they could look for somewhere else to live.

Doris was worried. How could she carry on with her sittings with the constant noise of construction going on? For a while, she played with the idea of moving into the caravan full time but quickly realised its small size and remote location would make it impractical. They dithered for months. Then one day, accidentally coming across the Oracle channel that their son Terry had set up on their TV, Doris noticed a house advertised for sale. It was nearer to Kent than Fulham but the price was surprisingly reasonable. She reckoned that if they sold the caravan and committed their life savings, for the first time in their lives they might be able to buy a property. Which is how, in 1984, at the age of 64, Doris finally ended up with her own home.

That house in a leafy suburban street not far from Lewisham Theatre was Doris' pride and joy. Yet, it was by no means a mansion. Despite reports in the press that suggested Doris must be a millionaire, the house she bought was a modest semi, built around the 1930's, with a strip of garden at the front and a larger patch at the back, identical to millions of other ordinary suburban homes around the country.

Simply buying a property was revolutionary enough; Doris hadn't given any thought to doing it up. The Stokes family had never had much need to learn about interior design and furnishings. So one chaotic day in the flat, we all helped to pack their old belongings into tea-chests (somehow I clumsily managed to knock over and break a large china Shire horse. 'Don't worry luv. Doesn't matter a bit,' Doris assured me) fully expecting them to be on display in the new house, very soon.

But when her old friends at Woman's Own heard of Doris' change of address, they offered to redecorate the place for her (to feature in the magazine of course). So, for quite a while, the tea-chests remained unpacked in the garage. Eventually, many weeks later, the house emerged shiny and new and far grander than Doris could ever have envisaged.

'Isn't it lovely!' she said beaming, when I visited for the first time. It was ideal. The outside was painted sky blue and white; there were cottage-style leaded light windows, and roses blooming in the front garden. Yet inside, despite some elaborate swagged curtains and designery touches, the feel was still very much like Doris' old flat. We stood at the door to the front room to admire the new wallpaper, the impressive curtains, and what looked like some very highly polished new furniture, but we didn't go in. There hadn't been a second reception room in the flat and you got the feeling Doris didn't quite know what to do with this one. It was clearly for 'best'. It didn't look as if it would get much use.

'Come out Boots!' she said firmly as the little dog dashed past our feet to rush in. Then she shut the door and we moved on into the back where the family actually lived. Doris' armchair was positioned beside the fire and facing the window, just like in the flat. Only this window was full length and overlooked the garden where a bird table had been set up. I'm not sure how many years it had been since Doris lived in a home with a garden, but after so long in the flat, her very own plot gave her enormous pleasure. She loved to watch the birds pecking at the strings of peanuts that swung from the feeder, and she was thrilled to find there was such a thing as a blue rose.

'Can you imagine? A rose that's Blue!' she told me when she heard about it. 'It's called Blue Moon.' Of course, she had to have one. She made frequent trips down the garden to admire it when it was in flower and she always pointed it out to visitors. In truth, it looked more pale lavender than blue to me, but Doris loved it all the same.

Her board of spirit children had also survived the move. Doris wasn't able to do many private sittings these days, so she prioritised parents who, like herself, had lost children. Often, the parents would bring along photographs of their son or daughter, and Doris would pin these up on a large board in the sitting room. She made sure a vase of fresh flowers was always positioned in front of the board – 'for the children' – and she seemed to know the name of every young face.

All in all, everything was going well for Doris with the possible exception of her health. There were more cancer scares, she suffered a mini-stroke, and she seemed to catch every bug going. Yet, her career trajectory and workload was staggering. By now, she was virtually a household name; she regularly packed out the largest and most prestigious theatres, she demonstrated her abilities on radio phone-ins and in interviews, she was the subject of Desert Island Discs, and a Forty Minutes documentary, and celebrities were eager to meet her.

Doris, who was completely star-struck, was thrilled when her favourite actors from Coronation Street called to say 'hello', and when comedians and TV presenters wanted to make her acquaintance. She couldn't understand why, but she was delighted all the same and revelled in their chats. She became a shameless name-dropper and regaled her readers with news of her latest celebrity encounters. She wasn't intending to impress, though, she was simply sharing her excitement, as one fan to another.

She even created her own informal 'Sod-It' Club – for people like her, who had survived cancer. Quite a few celebrities joined the ranks, as well as countless lesser-known patients. The name was not an acronym – it was Sod-it as in: 'Sod it, I'm not going to have it!' which was what she found herself saying after yet another gloomy consultation with a doctor. She decided a defiant yet upbeat approach was the best plan when faced with depressing news, and it wasn't long before other sufferers were inspired to adopt the idea. Various low-key support groups began to form, some with and some without contact with Doris. She encouraged them all.

Yet still – despite the fame and the fuss – Doris remained unchanged, or so she appeared to me. Perhaps it was because success came so late in life or maybe it was her strong sense of self and deeply engrained philosophy. Maybe it was Ramanov's stern presence. Whatever the reason, Doris was still noticeably the same the woman I'd met all those years before, walking through the washing lines.

'She treated everyone the same,' Tony Ortzen agreed. 'She genuinely did. Whether they were a Duke or a dustman, it made no difference to Doris. She treated them exactly the same.'

'She even invited my wife and me to Psychic News dinner dances and to her book launch party,' recalled theatre manager Chris Hare. 'I can't think of any other artists who would have done that.'

Yet while famous faces made Doris giddy as a teenage autograph hunter, she was not impressed by wealth. She was well aware that there were things far more important than money.

I remember one morning when we were working; a millionaire phoned from his palatial home in Switzerland.

After the call Doris put the phone down with a sigh, 'That man's spent his health to get his wealth,' she said, shaking her head. 'Now he's trying to spend his wealth to get his health. But it can't be done...' She could offer him comfort, but she knew she couldn't help him. Doris seldom criticised, but it was clear she thought he'd made the wrong choice.

So, Doris remained unchanged. It was her strength but perhaps it was her weakness too. She couldn't help behaving the way she'd always behaved and doing things the way she'd always done them. Essentially, to Doris, the theatre appearances were the same as her appearances in the Spiritualist churches of the north all those years before, just on a grander scale and shorn of religious content.

But that's not how they were viewed by others. The more high profile she became, the more unwelcome the attention she attracted.

These days Wikipedia records that she was a controversial figure, described by some as: 'The Gracie Fields of the psychic world' and others as 'A ruthless, money-making con artist.' It also suggests that it's been 'established' that Doris planted unwitting accomplices in the audience to receive 'messages', and also that she picked up information about audience members by having staff eavesdrop in the theatre queue before the show, then relaying the information to her before she went on stage.

Such accusations infuriated Laurie. 'If they're saying she's a fraud, they're saying I'm a fraud too,' he said at the time. 'Because none of that could have happened without me knowing or being involved. I'm not a fraud, and it's totally untrue that we planted people in the audience.'

In fact, later, after Doris passed away, Laurie was offered a large sum by the press to expose her as a fake.

'But I couldn't do it even if I wanted the money,' said Laurie. 'Because there was nothing to expose. I know she wasn't a fraud.'

In the early years, too, Andre Ptaszynski was aware of the possibility of unwelcome accusations.

'As she became well known, people began to send letters to the theatres for her,' he recalled. 'And when they were handed to her, Doris would read them.'

Although there was no suggestion Doris then went on to give messages to the letter writers, Andre moved quickly to forestall any problems. 'I put a stop to it,' he said. 'I stopped her getting letters handed in at the stage door until after the show. To be fair, Doris was very relaxed about it and it didn't seem to make any difference to the evening. In fact, in the end, I began to feel a bit guilty about it.'

The trouble was, critics and the press started from the point of view that what Doris claimed to be doing was obviously impossible. Since no one could do the impossible, Doris' apparently impressive results could only be achieved by trickery. Given that it was impossible for Doris to be genuine, they reasoned, then logically, no matter how nice she seemed, she must be a fraud. Therefore, it was their mission to discover how she did it and unmask her.

This was completely understandable, predictable even, but Doris couldn't see it. Or at least she could when it was pointed out to her, but she was hurt by the unkind words and found it extremely difficult to stop doing what came naturally. Every day she received sackfuls of desperate letters and dozens of imploring phone calls from people who somehow obtained her home number. She couldn't possibly see all the people who begged for sittings – there were thousands of them – yet their tragic stories troubled her. So she did what she would have done all those years before, when she was just another unknown medium from the local spiritualist church.

'Why don't you come along to the church on Sunday?' she'd say. 'You might get a message.'

Only now it might be, 'I'm not doing any private sittings at the moment, but I'm going to be at your local theatre next month. Why don't you come along? You might get a message.'

So, as her fame grew, the chances were that at any theatre, on any given night, there may be a few people in the audience who'd previously spoken to Doris. There were also devoted fans who followed Doris from theatre to theatre and had seen her many times, possibly talked to her at the stage door after a show, and got her autograph. If some of them then received a message, this would look to a reporter very much like collusion. It could look as if they were planted accomplices – either witting or unwitting.

Laurie was aware of this and tried to stop Doris suggesting to fans that they might like to come to her theatre appearances.

'But it was so difficult,' said Ellen Frazer Jameson who accompanied Doris on many theatre tours. Multi-talented Ellen – author of a series of romance novels including Love Kills with a Kiss, journalist, broadcaster, actress and theatre director now based in Miami – met Doris through her late husband, the legendary newspaper editor and broadcaster Derek Jameson. 'Derek met Doris when they were both on TV-am one morning,' recalled Ellen. 'Doris had always been nervous of being in the press and thought Derek was there to challenge her, but in fact they hit it off immediately. They'd both known great poverty when they were young; they were both down to earth characters and they had a natural affinity.

'Anyway, they got along so well Doris invited Derek and myself to a Psychic News dinner dance that was coming up. Of course, I hadn't met Doris at this point so I was a bit nervous to find I was seated next to her at the table. We'd hardly sat down when she turned to me and said 'I've got your mother here and she's saying, 'Show me the ring then. Let's see the ring!''

Ellen was astonished. Derek was a high profile celebrity at the time, frequently written about in the gossip columns and the couple had been trying to keep their relationship private. 'We'd secretly got engaged in Tenerife not long before,' said Ellen, 'and Derek had given me a beautiful ring with a green volcanic stone which we'd found in a local store. No one knew. Certainly not Doris. And Doris couldn't have known that my mother had passed away. But, of course, that's exactly what my mother would have said. She would have been very keen to see my new engagement ring.'

It wasn't the time or the place to delve any further but Ellen arranged to visit Doris at her Fulham flat the following week for a proper sitting. This must have been in the months before the Stokes moved away from Sir Oswald Stoll Mansions because Ellen recalls there was such a terrible din from building work, going on in the other blocks, that Doris didn't think anything would happen.

'Then suddenly she said, 'Hang on. Is your mother called Amy?' 'Mamie, I said,' replied Ellen, 'And she was off. Family names, details, the fact my father was in the RAF, and so on. Doris who'd been a WRAF herself during the war, asked what rank he was. 'Your mum says, 'Well you'd have had to call him Chiefie, dear,' Doris told me. Which was true. Dad was an officer. Afterwards, at home, Derek and I talked it over and we agreed that either Doris had spent a fortune having me followed and checked out, which was highly unlikely, or she'd got a hotline to upstairs!'

Since Derek was a tabloid journalist who'd edited the Daily Mirror, Daily Express, and the Daily Star, he knew better than most how difficult and expensive it would have been to discover so many personal background details about a relative unknown like Ellen, particularly in such a short time – in these days before the internet. For this reason, he was satisfied Doris was genuine.

From then on, the couple became great friends of the family and when Tony Ortzen was unable to travel from London to assist at Doris' more distant theatre tours, Ellen – with her stage background – was able to step into the role.

She travelled with Doris and John, stayed at the hotels with them, and generally helped sort out 1001 little behind-the-scenes details, as well as actually performing the introduction on stage.

'When people said Doris must be memorising all those details she gave out at the theatre, they have no idea how impossible it would have been,' said Ellen. 'Wherever she was, from the moment she woke up till the time she went to bed, people were finding excuses to come to her room or walk down the corridor with her, in the hope of getting a message. The chambermaid, the waiters and waitresses, the room service boys, the hairdresser, the woman who did her nails, the staff on reception – there was a constant stream of people, all hoping for a few words. She got no rest. They'd queue up outside the door, just waiting for the smallest excuse to come in. And quite often Doris would have an accurate personal message for them, just like the one from my mother about the ring. And the same thing would happen when we got to the theatre. Backstage, everyone gravitated to Doris hoping for a word. With all that going on it would have been impossible to memorise a whole series of specific details to bring out later.'

Then there were the letters. Wherever Doris happened to be, fans would find out where she was staying and send letters to the hotel as well as the theatre. Laurie had tried to ban Doris from reading letters in advance to avoid any accusations in the press, so it fell to Ellen to deal with the post.

'The letters were devastating,' said Ellen. 'They made me so sad. One day after reading through a whole stream of tragic stories I came across one that was even worse than usual, and I started to cry.

'What's wrong?' asked Doris. 'Your job's so heart-breaking,' I told her. 'All this tragedy. I don't know how you do it.' And she sat down next to me on the sofa to comfort me. 'Are you talking about the little black girl with lots of little braids and beads in her hair? I can see her sitting beside you. I'd say she was about seven.' I looked back at the letter I'd just opened – which Doris had not seen or even touched. 'She's eight actually!' I teased. She had her 8th birthday two days before she died. It turned out she'd been murdered by her father, who was now in prison, and her mother was hoping for a sitting with Doris.

'Phone her and see if she'd like to come to the theatre,' said Doris. Then she stopped. 'No, you'd better not. You know what they'll say. They'll say it's collusion.' But we couldn't ignore the poor woman. So, instead, I phoned her and told her what Doris had seen. The mum confirmed her little girl looked exactly as Doris had described and she seemed to find it comforting.'

Ellen can recall no instances of helpers eavesdropping in theatre queues, of information being passed to Doris before she went on stage, or even of Doris memorising notes in her dressing room.

Certainly, when I was backstage in Lewisham I saw nothing like this going on. What's more, critics who claimed that such tactics accounted for Doris' accuracy during theatre shows, never seemed to have an explanation for how she could be just as successful during radio phone-ins.

'She was brilliant at phone-ins,' recalled broadcaster Ed Doolan of BBC WM in Birmingham at the time. 'One hundred percent straight up and she came on my show many times. But that first time, in between all the stuff she was getting for callers, she kept telling me about my father. 'He's got the same name as you,' she said. Which was true. And, 'He's talking about a birthday. Why's this birthday important?' 'Well he died on my birthday,' I said. I was amazed.'

On another occasion, Ed thought it would be interesting to stand Doris in front of a random, live audience and put out whatever happened – good or bad – live on air.

'I announced the idea on the show one lunchtime,' said Ed. 'And asked any listeners interested in being in the audience to apply by the next day. The first 150 would be chosen.'

When he arrived the next morning, there were 700 applications waiting. Any kind of collusion with Doris would have been out of the question unless the BBC set it up.

'Well, the show was extraordinary,' said Ed. 'The first ten to fifteen minutes weren't so good but then Doris seemed to settle down and she got hot. She was brilliant. The best I think she'd ever done.'

Yet, Doris didn't reserve her insights purely for broadcasts. One evening, on a visit to Birmingham, she and Ed were sitting chatting when the news came through that a prominent local MP, Jocelyn Cadbury, the young Member of Parliament for Birmingham Northfield, had just been found dead. It seemed as if he'd committed suicide.

'I'd only interviewed Jocelyn Cadbury the week before,' said Ed, 'so naturally I wondered what had happened, but the police hadn't released any more details. Then suddenly as we chatted, Doris said she'd got Jocelyn Cadbury through. 'He says he put a gun in his mouth and pulled the trigger,' Doris told us. We had no way of knowing if this was right or wrong but later – when the full story came out – we discovered that's exactly what happened.

'When Doris was on form, she was extraordinary. I wouldn't say she was always right, but by God, she wasn't often wrong.'

That was the other thing about Doris – her performances could be patchy.

'Some nights, she was definitely better than others, 'said Ellen. 'And with mothers who'd lost children particularly, she was brilliant. She seemed to have an affinity with them. If she was a fraud, you'd have expected her to be more or less the same every time, and she wasn't.

But whether she was at her best, or not quite so good, there's no doubt she brought a lot of joy to a lot of people. She gave them a solace they couldn't find anywhere else.'

Nevertheless, her theatre appearances continued to attract controversy. Various magicians scoffed and claimed her performances were simple trickery which they themselves could produce with ease.

'One was particularly vocal,' said Doris. 'So I invited him to come to my next theatre and come up on stage with me. I said I'd do my bit and then he could do the same – his way – and we'd see what happened. He never took me up on it.'

None of them ever did.

CHAPTER 9

The extraordinary thing was that Doris looked so good. After months of ill health – dizzy spells, excruciating ear-ache, and a baffling collapse – during which she looked sadly unwell and exhausted, here she was sitting up in her hospital bed surrounded by enough flowers to stock a florist's shop and smiling brightly.

After her second collapse, Doris had finally been diagnosed with a brain tumour – and clearly it couldn't have developed overnight. Perhaps this was why she'd been having such difficulty remembering things as we recorded the anecdotes for her latest book. Despite the fact that she continued working – dosed up with painkillers and gallons of hot tea and seemed as accurate in her readings as ever – quite often these days she couldn't remember afterwards what she'd said. So, if she wanted to include a particularly interesting case in her book, she'd get me to phone the people involved to hear the details from them directly. She knew they'd remember what she'd told them far better than she would herself.

In retrospect, it also showed how impossible it would have been for Doris to memorise huge chunks of material in order to fake her theatre shows, as critics so often accused her of doing. Her brain simply wouldn't have been up to it.

The tumour was operable, Doris had been told, and she was scheduled for surgery.

'They're going to have to shave part of my hair off, round here,' said Doris running her hand over the springy curls just above one ear, 'It'll take ages to grow back, so I'll just have to wear a turban for a while. I've asked Laurie to get me a few, in different colours – don't want to frighten people!'

She sounded quite cheerful, but I was deeply worried. My mind flew back to a conversation just a few months before. We were working on Doris' seventh book and sitting in the back room of the lovely new house. Doris was in her big armchair overlooking the garden, watching the birds flitting back and forth to the bird table as she talked. After a while, we took a break for our usual sandwich lunch.

'D'you know,' said Doris thoughtfully, 'the other day I was watching TV when I heard this spirit voice.'

Doris often talked of the spirit voices she heard so this wasn't a particularly surprising comment. I carried on eating.

'And it said,' she went on, 'your time on earth is over, your life in spirit is begun, when you stand before the Master we know he'll say 'well done' … Isn't that beautiful? What a lovely epitaph...'

The sandwich almost fell from my fingers. The expression 'my blood ran cold' hit home. Suddenly, I understood what it meant. I didn't think the rhyme was beautiful, it struck me as extremely alarming, yet Doris didn't appear to take it personally. She often received simple lines of verse in this way. She found them comforting and shared them with her readers. She appeared to view this latest rhyme in the same light.

'Wouldn't it be wonderful to feel you'd earned an epitaph like that?' she said.

I could only nod, in a non-committal way, and hope the words weren't some kind of prediction.

It was 1987. Margaret Thatcher was prime minister, Ronald Reagan president of the USA. Shoulder pads and big hair jostled down the streets, and substantial numbers of us women painted our nails red, slashed on scarlet lipstick, and tried to strut about like the outrageously arrogant 'superbitch', Alexis, played by Joan Collins in the

TV show of the moment, Dynasty. A black velvet chequebook cover (remember chequebooks?) with the words 'Rich Bitch' picked out in glittering diamantes on the front was the 'must-have' accessory of the moment.

Most of this, with the possible exception of Margaret Thatcher, a fellow Grantham girl, would have passed Doris by of course, though she wasn't averse to watching rival glamour-soaps Dynasty and Dallas on TV like everyone else. What did catch her eye though was the big news story of March that year – the tragic ferry disaster in which a roll-on roll-off ferry – The Herald of Free Enterprise – capsized and sank outside Zeebrugge harbour in Belgium, killing 193 people. Some passengers somehow survived the appalling nightmare, only to find the other members of their party hadn't been so lucky. Some lost their whole families.

Like everyone else, Doris was horrified. So, when (just a few weeks later) a couple who'd lost their son in the catastrophe got in touch asking for a sitting, she agreed to see them, despite the fact she was obviously unwell.

I happened to be there when the Harrison family arrived. Doris had greeted me a few minutes earlier, pale and drawn and still in her dressing-gown. She felt so ill with such a bad pain in her head she'd actually tried to stop us all from coming as she didn't think she'd be able to work. But in those days before mobile phones, we were all on our way and couldn't be contacted.

As it turned out, this was to be the last full-length sitting Doris ever did, though, knowing her, she was probably giving little mini-readings to the nurses in the hospital before her operation. Despite her worries, Doris seemed to find her voices quite quickly that morning. She soon identified the Harrison's son – Stuart – who was only 17 when he took that fateful trip on the Herald of Free Enterprise. It turned out he'd only gone to please his friends. Carol Harrison, Stuart's mum, recorded the whole session and she was so pleased with how things turned out that, afterwards, she gave permission for the transcript to be printed in Doris' book *Joyful Voices*. She left the house grateful and smiling and seemed much happier than when she arrived.

Doris sank back in her chair, worn out but relieved she'd managed to battle through to the end. The doctor was on his way, and I left her to rest and hopefully recuperate.

Sadly, it wasn't to be. Little more than a week later Doris collapsed again and ended up in hospital, where the brain tumour was diagnosed.

Though outwardly she seemed cheerful and optimistic in her comfortable private room – organised as ever by the tireless Laurie – it's clear she was having doubts.

When I arrived, Derek Jameson and his wife Ellen were already there, sitting on the end of the bed laughing and chatting. They'd brought her a teddy bear for luck.

But, afterwards, Derek told me that, as he was leaving, Doris became upset.

'Derek, it's not that I'm afraid of passing over,' she told him, clinging to his hand, 'I know that can only bring joy and happiness. But what's so upsetting is I haven't done half the things I wanted to do. It's only in the last couple of years I've been able to enjoy the good things in life, and now it's all being taken away.'

The next day, on the morning of the operation, Laurie found her in a similar mood.

'You know I'm not afraid of dying,' she told him when he asked what was troubling her. 'No, what I'm afraid of is what if it goes wrong? It's a very delicate operation.

'If it goes wrong, what good would I be to anyone? I wouldn't be able to work, and that's all I do isn't it? If I can't do that Laurie, what good would I be?'

As a former nurse, Doris understood the risks she faced. She feared she might be left blind, or deaf, or brain-damaged, or possibly unable to speak.

'Doris Stokes you've done too much good for the spirit world for them to do that to you,' said Laurie, who had a wonderful knack of saying the right thing at the right time. 'But if you do leave us and go into the spirit world – don't put voices in my ear. I don't want them! I can manage you as a medium, but I don't want to <u>be</u> a medium!'

There was a pause, then Doris burst out laughing, and she was still chuckling as the nurses came to wheel her away.

And who knows, perhaps she'd already been thinking about what would happen if... After all, as she joked so many times, 'You can't die for the life of you.'

David Chapman, now a medium himself, recalls how he encountered Doris unexpectedly during her last hospital stay.

'I was working in St John's Wood, London, at the time,' said David, 'and one day, the radio was on, and a newsflash suddenly interrupted the show. It said that Doris Stokes had been taken to a hospital in St John's Wood. I was amazed. I knew the place, and it was just up the road from where I was at that moment.'

David had been a fan ever since he won tickets in a magazine competition to a Doris Stokes show at the Barbican Theatre. He and his wife had been so impressed with their free evening, and enjoyed it so much, they promptly booked to see Doris again at the Palladium.

'One exchange stands out in my mind particularly,' said David. 'The Palladium is arranged in tier after tier of seats rising up towards the heavens. Doris explained she could see a light over people's heads, which meant her message was for them. Well, way up in the heavens, she suddenly called to a man in the rows way above: 'Hello love, Is your name 'Ted'?' (I've used the name Ted as I can't recall exactly.) He said yes. She said 'I think I've got your wife here and then she gave the lady's name. Ted replied with a firm yes, so Doris said come on down to the front of the stage. Take your time.'

David recalls that Doris continued giving messages to other people while Ted made his laborious way down numerous flights of stairs.

'When he finally arrived,' David went on, 'Doris said, 'Hello my dear, your wife is saying sorry she left you in the night. She says she walked for miles in her dressing gown... And she was found in water.' Ted confirmed this was true. 'She also says that because of her illness, she didn't want you to have the burden of looking after her, so she left in the middle of the night.' Tears started to flow, but Doris went on with many more names. Then, right at the end, she said suddenly: 'And you still carry her wedding ring – in your right pocket!' 'I do,' said Ted and he put his hand in his pocket and brought out the ring to show her. There was great applause.'

Even more impressed, David would have liked to stay behind to have a few words with Doris but realised the crowds were too great. He'd never get near her. So he and his wife went home, and David accepted he'd probably never get an opportunity to speak to Doris in person.

'So a few months later, when I heard on the radio she was so close by, well I decided I had to go over to see her,' he said. 'I went out and bought some flowers and a card and dashed over to the hospital. I went to the reception desk asking for Doris Stokes. They said no one with that name here, then one of them said there is a Doris Fisher. I said 'Yes, that's the one!'

Luckily David had remembered that, on her earliest book, Doris' name was printed as Doris Fisher Stokes. It couldn't be a coincidence, David reasoned. Sure enough, he was directed to a room on the second floor and as soon as he reached the corridor he knew he was in the right place.

'As I approached the door, I saw all these bouquets and sprays of flowers laying on the floor outside. They were so beautiful, and there was me with this small bundle of flowers which were already dropping. I felt so out of place.'

As he stood there deliberating whether to put down the flowers or not, the door suddenly opened. 'A nurse was just coming out. She looked at the flowers in my hand and said: 'Are those for Doris?' I said yes. 'You'd better come in and give them to her then,' she said.'

Seconds later, David found himself face to face with Doris in her hospital bed. Awkwardly, he gave her the flowers and the card.

'Doris, God can't take you,' I said without thinking,' recalled David, 'You've got so much work to do.' And she said: 'Lovey, I'll work from spirit and I'll work with children.'

So, perhaps, in a way she'd already sensed the outcome and was planning ahead.

Yet, that afternoon – the afternoon before her operation – she was putting on a brave face for her visitors. An optimistic face. It was Friday and the operation was scheduled for Saturday. 'Oh well. On Sunday I'll either be here or I won't,' she said jauntily.

I didn't like it.

When it was time for me to go, I struggled to find the right words. If only Laurie had been there to help me out. I was so worried, but wanted to keep things light. The book we'd just completed was the first book in a two-book contract. We had committed to providing the publishers with a second manuscript within the year, so: 'Come on Doris, you've got to be ok,' I said, 'We've got another book to write. Don't drop me in it! I can't do it without you!'

Our eyes met. Yet, oddly, I can't remember what she said. Perhaps she didn't reply. She just smiled. And that's the last I saw of her.

The next day the operation took place. It took six-and-a-half hours, and I believe it was a success. Sadly, though, Doris never regained consciousness. She slipped quietly away 13 days later on May 8th. Some weeks afterwards, David Chapman came across a comforting post-script.

'I was reading Psychic News and a story caught my eye,' he said. 'It was about a little girl who'd been very ill in a coma. Her mother was by her bedside when, unexpectedly, she started to open her eyes and she came round. Her mother was so overjoyed. Then, after a while, when the little girl was able to speak, she said: 'I was helped by a lady in white.' Her mother just was so thankful that her daughter was out of this coma, she didn't take much notice. But, at the time, the papers were full of stories about Doris Stokes and what could have happened to all the money the media believed she had. Anyway, the little girl pointed to her mother's newspaper and said: 'There's the lady in white who helped me.' The mother looked at the picture she was pointing at. It was a photo of Doris.'

For David, that story confirmed Doris was as good as her word. She had fulfilled her promise. She hadn't stopped working. She was still busy – helping children, from the other side.

CHAPTER 10

Even in 1987, Islington – once a faded, down-at-heel London borough – was moving swiftly upmarket, and residential Highbury New Park turned out to be particularly pleasant. Big, old London Plane trees with dappled trunks lined both sides of the road; rustling canopies meeting high overhead in a great green tunnel. It was a wonderfully shady place to walk on a warm summer's day.

A few months had now passed since the spring, and Doris' sad death (although, of course, she would have hated the word death. 'You can't die for the life of you,' I could almost hear her voice correcting me in my head), and I was still struggling to adjust. As well as missing her comforting personality and joyous sense of humour, the media aftermath following her sudden demise was proving difficult to handle.

The name Doris Stokes kept popping up in the news – and not in a good way. The press couldn't get over the fact that she appeared not to have accumulated the enormous wealth they were certain she must have possessed. Stories about the mystery of her missing millions kept appearing in the papers, and there were dark hints about secret Swiss bank accounts and offshore companies. They simply could not believe she gave away most of her earnings, and that – knowing Doris – she'd much sooner have had a Swiss roll than a Swiss bank account any day.

I stepped around a dustbin left carelessly across the pavement. The street was such an odd mix of gentrification and gothic decay. Intriguing Victorian villas set well back from the road basked quietly in the sunshine, but while some were sleek and recently renovated, others were gently crumbling – half-hidden by high walls, untamed foliage, and a jumble of old mattresses and discarded prams.

The road was strangely deserted too. Considering this was the centre of London, it was surprisingly quiet. Few cars disturbed the hazy peace and there was not another soul to be seen. Friends used to joke about me being a medium's ghost, but now, as I drifted along the empty pavement under the whispering trees, I felt a bit ghostlike too. Doris was gone, I reminded myself, and it was time to move on. Yet what I didn't realise then was that now I was no longer Doris' ghost – in a sense, she was about to become mine.

As time passed, I thought I was walking further and further away from the Doris Stokes phenomenon – only to discover, years later, I'd been going round in a circle.

People with unusual abilities – little echoes of Doris' – kept crossing my path like beads on a string, each one unknowingly revealing another strand of the mystery. And as the decades slipped by, the intervals between these meetings grew shorter and shorter until, at last, I found I was back at the beginning – with Doris Stokes centre stage once again.

I was totally unaware of all this that particular day in North London, of course. There was no way of knowing, then, that I was on my way to meet the first of them – these Doris outriders – that very afternoon in the exuberant shape of palmist Bettina Luxon.

Bettina had been commissioned to write a book on the ancient study of hands, I'd been told. Like Doris, she'd benefited from very little education as a child, so she wasn't confident of her way with the written word. She'd read Voices in My Ear, though, and despite the fact the Voices series were autobiographies and Bettina was embarking on a factual book, for some reason she was inspired to contact Doris' publishers to ask if I could help her.

I knew nothing about palmistry and could see no logical reason to explain how it could possibly work. Yet, I was curious to learn that Bettina's commission came from a business publisher. Surely palmistry was all about crossing palms with silver and discovering tall, dark, handsome strangers? What could it possibly have to offer the clear-sighted, cut-throat world of business?

Yet, perhaps, the idea wasn't as crazy as it sounded. This was the era in which the astonishing news broke that the then-president of the USA, Ronald Reagan, was in the habit of consulting an astrologer for advice on how to run the country.

It seemed like a joke when we first heard the rumours, and it caused much merriment and TV satire. Today, we'd assume it was 'fake news'. Yet, as unbelievable as the stories sounded, further information gradually emerged, and it became clear they contained more than an element of truth. Ronald's wife Nancy, it seemed, had met astrologer Joan Quigley years before, and after an assassination attempt on the president's life in 1981, Nancy began to consult her on a regular basis.

'Not since the days of the Roman Emperors and never in the history of the United States presidency,' Joan wrote later in her autobiography, 'has an astrologer played such a significant role in the nation's affairs of State.'

And the president's Chief of Staff, confusingly named Donald Regan, complained later in his own memoirs: 'Virtually every major move and decision the Reagans made during my time as White House Chief of Staff was cleared in advance with a woman in San Francisco [Quigley] who drew up horoscopes to make certain the planets were in a favourable alignment for the enterprise.'

Mr. Regan obviously disapproved but, clearly, there was something in the air.

'Oh yes,' Rosemary Burr of Roster's business publishers, who'd commissioned Bettina's book, told me later. 'It may sound unlikely but businessmen, though they say they deal only in logic and facts, are some of the most superstitious people you could meet.

'Despite all the statistics and theories, no one can really tell in advance which business will succeed and which will fail. If they could, none would ever lose money. Although they like to take the credit for their foresight if they're successful, deep down they know there's a lot of luck involved. You'd be surprised how many apparently cynical business people secretly turn to astrologers and psychics for advice.'

Rosemary was so convinced of this; she was prepared to publish Bettina's book on the subject.

I checked the Luxon address again. Much as I'd love to have a peek inside one of those atmospheric villas, I knew it wasn't to be. Bettina had explained she lived in a purpose-built flat and there – across the road, sandwiched between the grand homes – I could see a plain, no-frills block that just had to be the place.

I hurried up the stairs to the first floor and knocked. Bettina Luxon turned out to be a bright, bird-like woman with short black curls and vivid blue eyes sparkling with mischief. Her age was a closely guarded secret. 'Never tell anyone you're over fifty,' she advised me cheerfully. 'No matter what they say, they won't take you seriously if they think you're old.' So, for all the years I knew her, Bettina remained around the age of fifty – although she enjoyed an annual birthday every January without getting a day older. She shamelessly knocked at least ten years off her age on the rare occasions anyone enquired, but no one ever challenged her. And, in truth, she had such a vibrant, bubbly personality, she was eternally young.

Like Doris, Bettina had been born into a poor family and spent little time at school. She knew her palmistry backwards – even though, oddly, she appeared not to need it – but the vagaries of grammar and spelling were tricky for her.

'I've been fascinated by hands ever since I was tiny,' she explained. 'Even as a little girl, I saw that all hands are different.'

She began searching out books on palmistry in the library near her London home, and later began collecting tomes on the subject from second-hand book shops and jumble sales. As she compared the diagrams in the books with the hands she saw around her every day, she realised the old palmists were, at the very least, wonderful observers and they recorded the truth.

'Palmistry goes back thousands of years,' Bettina told me. 'The ancient Egyptians probably used palmistry, and their knowledge has been passed down throughout the centuries ever since.'

Bettina certainly knew the theory, and she had a number of regular clients who came for consultations at her flat. She could even work with photocopies of their handprints if they couldn't spare the time to visit.

'A great many of them are businessmen,' she said. 'They like to come and talk to me whenever there's a decision to be made. Sometimes they're not sure if they should agree to a particular deal or not, or if they're going in the right direction. There's a lot of trouble with partnerships too. Generally, I advise against going into partnerships – I've seen so many of them ending up with problems.'

Bettina would always start by studying a client's palm; to her, there was more to be seen than just the complex squiggle of lines visible to most observers.

I realised this when she took a look at my hand soon after we met and, after talking about relationships and career and so on, started describing the white cottage where I lived and the garden gate. All correct as it happened, but…

'Now Bettina,' I said. 'Where on earth on my palm is the line that shows a white cottage and a garden gate?'

She laughed. 'Well, actually no. There's not a line. I can see a picture. When I look in people's hands I often see pictures.'

I examined my palm more closely. Nope. No pictures of any kind, not even a smudge of biro could be seen. Just a cob-webby network of baffling lines (a sign of an overactive mind and born worrier, as I know now!) And I can truthfully admit that I've never once seen a picture in my palm, or anyone else's.

Yet Bettina's unusual combination of pictures and lines seemed to work for her. Her clients were delighted with her readings and though strangers often scoffed, they were still fascinated by what their palms might reveal.

Wherever we went while working on the book – in shops, offices, and social gatherings – people would flock to Bettina's side as soon as they heard what she did. 'What d'you see? What does my hand show?' they'd ask, eagerly thrusting their palms under her nose. She would usually oblige with some titbit of personal information that made them gasp.

It reminded me very much of the effect Doris had on the rare occasions we were out in public. Complete strangers would find any excuse to come over and strike up a conversation. Some were clearly desperate, others just curious, but all hoped Doris would say something meaningful to them. And, of course, she had a friendly word for them all.

It was particularly odd the way even declared sceptics couldn't resist making an approach.

'I don't believe in any of this,' said one man, pushing his way through the crowd when Bettina was invited to visit a business exhibition. 'But go on then, if you reckon you can do it – what can you see there?' and he waved a meaty hand in her face.

Bettina took a polite look and made a few diplomatic comments. For a moment, he seemed surprised, but then his belligerent manner returned. 'Oh yes, well that's right I s'pose, as far as it goes. But anyone could have said that…' He started to return his palm to Bettina for more but, fortunately, our host then arrived and whisked her away.

'Why did you bother with him? He was so rude,' I said as we headed to the next stand.

Bettina shrugged. 'It's funny. Even the ones that say they don't believe. Deep down, they're not quite sure... they want me to prove them wrong. Yet they don't. Doris had to put up with much worse, I'm sure.'

That was true. Bettina never drew my attention to it, but stories still appeared from time to time on the subject of how Doris purportedly faked her appearances. Theatre shows were dismissed as being achieved with an audience full of plants, while private readings, simply the result of manipulating the emotions of the bereaved.

How, as an ordinary housewife and complete stranger in Australia, with no staff and little advance warning, she managed to fill the Sydney Opera House with audience plants three nights in a row was never addressed. Neither was the subject of how she managed, repeatedly, to fake live BBC radio phone-ins.

Laurie, meanwhile, was offered large sums to expose Doris as a fraud, while it was suggested to me that I should claim

Doris was now contacting me from beyond the grave and giving me messages! Obviously, she wasn't, and I didn't.

It was immensely frustrating. But perhaps Bettina was right. Maybe the controversy lingered on partly because the sceptics couldn't leave it alone. They were sure they were right, of course, but did they (secretly) half want to be proved wrong?

One new colleague of mine, on hearing that my latest project involved palmistry, asked if he could have a reading with Bettina. I was surprised, as he didn't seem the superstitious type. I'd have put him down as one of the scoffers, but I organised a meeting for him with Bettina all the same. Afterwards, he emerged shaken but impressed.

'Blimey!' he said. 'She knew all about me. There was no fooling her. She picked up on my girlfriend, well both of them, and the fact I haven't told my wife... And I know you didn't tell her because you didn't know!'

Which was true. In fact, I was a bit shocked. I thought he was a happily married man!

After working with Doris for so long, it wasn't difficult for me to accept or even find particularly unusual that some people could do and see things most of us can't. So, I was quite prepared to believe Bettina was psychic and had flashes of accurate inspiration about people. What I wasn't prepared for was to find some truth in beliefs about palmistry – and that you didn't need to be psychic to learn a lot about a person from their hands.

I'd assumed the theory was all made up. Yet as we worked on the business book and Bettina began by describing different hand types – their shapes and the sizes – I found myself noticing the hands of people around me as I never had before. Just as she said, it was obvious their hands were so very different from each other. The variation was astonishing. No two hands were the same, and once you started noticing, it was difficult to stop.

'People with short fingers tend to be impatient, action lovers,' said Bettina, 'whereas people with long, slim fingers tend to be the look-before-they-leap types. They take their time and research into things. They like detail.'

As I compared her theories with the hands of the people I knew, I couldn't help thinking, 'Well yes, they are like that.' And as the details built up, and Bettina explained the significance – according to the lores of palmistry – of more and more lines and markings, I was baffled to find that if I checked them against people I knew, the palmistry assessments were usually accurate.

For the purposes of the business book, we collected photographs of a number of the top businessmen of the day, selecting pictures where possible that showed the great men (usually men back then, I'm afraid) waving, so their entire hands were on display with the palm facing outwards.

We noticed, interestingly, that men who were chairmen of big corporations such as BT tended to have very similar hands, in which their first three fingers were almost the same length. This is quite an unusual hand shape, so to find it cropping up so frequently in men with similar jobs led Bettina to conclude that an unusual combination of particular qualities in equal quantities was required to reach the top of big corporations – and these men all possessed them.

Individuals who were successful in more informal, innovative, creative fields had quite different hand shapes, often hands in which the ring finger was longer, denoting artistic talents.

The more I looked at various hands, and compared their owners' personalities with the qualities palmists believed people with such hands would possess, the more intrigued I became. There did seem to be something in palmistry after all. I just couldn't fathom how or why this should be.

'People know it instinctively,' said Bettina. 'We talk of people being open-handed or tight-fisted, meaning they're generous or mean. And a person with something to hide will often put their hands in their pockets or out of sight because they sense their hands could reveal more about them than they want to share. Even the medical profession finds meaning in hands. Doctors check the hands of new-born babies for signs of possible Downs Syndrome.'

Whether or not they still do this I don't know, but apparently individuals with certain neurological conditions, including Down's Syndrome, often have an unusual palm print. Instead of three main lines on their palm – with one curling around the base of the thumb, and the other two running parallel to each other across the centre of the hand – these people have just two of the major lines, the curving line and one other. It's as if the two horizontal lines of the palm have fused together into one single line that runs right across the middle of the hand, from side to side.

Palmists call this line the Simian line. Around ten percent of the population have the Simian line in one hand only. 'When it's in just one hand, it shows a person who could be a genius,' Bettina said. 'Because they have the ability to throw themselves heart and soul into whatever interests them. If you have the power to concentrate all your energies so intensely, you can often be very successful.'

It's much more unusual to find the Simian line in both hands. When this does occur, it can sometimes indicate Down's syndrome.

Some hand readers refer to the palm as 'the visible part of the brain,' and the more I researched, the more I could see what they meant. Like many people, I'd assumed the three main lines on the palm were merely creases – formed by repeatedly opening and closing the fist. Yet technology has revealed these three major lines are actually formed in the tiny foetal hand, in the first 12 weeks after conception – just as the brain itself is beginning to develop.

As I did more research, I found that scientists were even discovering that certain finger lengths correlated with a talent for sport or music or art, while others suggested organisational skills.

All this was fascinating to Bettina, but not exactly news. 'Palmists have always believed a long ring finger is associated with ability in sport, dance, or similar,' she said, 'and also with a talent for subjects like maths, music, or art. Plus, we've always said a long index finger shows a person who's a good organiser. They're only saying what palmists have been saying all along.'

Bettina was convinced that science has only just begun to scratch the surface. But it made little difference to her. She knew what she knew, and she didn't need to know why.

'I had quite a few readings with Bettina,' recalled Ainslie MacLeod, a successful psychic himself, originally from Scotland but now living in the USA, 'and she was a huge influence on me. Almost every time I sat down with her, she'd take my hand and press my fingers, saying, "You're psychic, and you should be doing something with it." And I'd say, "If I was psychic, I wouldn't be paying you to do it!" It was like a ritual.

'She predicted a whole number of things that happened, including the death of my uncle (with a complete description of his home), and how I'd become a professional psychic after moving to America. Which I did, eventually, but at the time it seemed absurd. She was also instrumental in getting me out of a toxic relationship. Two toxic relationships actually!'

Ainslie rated Bettina highly at the time, but his admiration grew stronger as the years passed and he realised that even the predictions he'd previously dismissed as being wildly unlikely, were actually coming true. Other clients were equally impressed. Bettina found herself being recommended to their friends and business associates, she began to contribute to magazines, and she was even asked to give talks at the fashionable health spa, Champneys – once a favourite haunt of Princess Diana's, apparently, as well as a string of celebrities and super-models. The red brick mansion set in landscaped grounds in the Hertfordshire countryside, outside Tring, seemed the epitome of glamour. Bettina was very excited.

'Come with me!' she said. 'It'll be fun, and you might be able to write about it.'

So off we went to mingle with the wealthy, the cool, and the downright gorgeous. It was evening and Bettina had been designated a pleasant room with lush carpets, sweeping curtains, and tall windows that probably overlooked the lovely gardens, but it was too dark to see them. The house had once belonged to Lady Rothschild, we heard, and it retained an alluring air of luxury. Bettina took it all in, in delight. She was determined to enjoy every second.

Basically, she was to be the evening's entertainment for the exclusive guests… fatigued, perhaps, from a long day of massages, facials, and exercise sessions.

Bettina hadn't brought much in the way of props. It was just Bettina in her smartest trousers, top, and brave lipstick, standing in front of an easel adorned with a whiteboard on which she'd stuck a few sheets of paper with the outlines of hand shapes she'd drawn herself in black marker pen.

As we stood there, looking out over the empty rows of neat gold chairs with their pale velvet seats, our shoes sinking into the matching carpet, I began to wonder if this was all a horrible mistake. After all, Bettina wasn't a performer and she normally worked one-to-one with clients, often at her small Formica-topped kitchen table in the privacy of her flat. Surely this audience was used to more sophisticated fare?

But there was no time to back out now. Suddenly, there was the sound of voices in the hall. Dinner was clearly over. The doors opened and in trooped the guests. Some looked interested, others frankly bored, as if they'd been dragged in against their will. A number of James Bonds were rumoured to have graced these elegant rooms from time to time in the past, so with what (we hoped) was a nonchalant manner, we tried to check out the audience for famous faces. Unfortunately, tonight, none of them seemed familiar.

They took their time, picking their way between the seats. Some glanced at the whiteboard with mild curiosity; others just carried on chatting with their companions. Oh dear, I thought. How's Bettina going to manage this?

Yet she didn't seem too bothered. Once they were settled, she just introduced herself, explained that most people have three main lines on the palms of their hands and – taking out her black marker pen – began to draw them in on the hand shapes on her board.

The effect was astonishing. After a few minutes, even the most blasé audience members were sitting up and taking notice. In every row, people were examining their own hands, comparing palms with their neighbours and checking the board for the next piece of information. Soon, they were asking questions; Bettina was explaining the many variations to the basic lines they may have found on their palms, and then she was walking up and down the rows helping categorise some of the more perplexing markings. By the end of the evening, the room buzzing. Everyone wanted to chat with Bettina and also with each other. Hands were waving everywhere; people were trying to decipher each other's' palms. And of course, when the talk was finally over, they came crowding round, hoping for individual readings.

As always, Bettina gave mini-readings to everyone who asked. Strangely, I only ever saw her refuse a reading once.

Visiting an office for a meeting, some time after Champneys, she was besieged as usual with workers wanting their fortunes told. She moved through them, good-naturedly making small comments about each hand thrust towards her, just as she seemed to do everywhere she went. But then, she came to the hand of a woman I knew well. This lady was popular, highly-talented, and seemed to have an exciting future in front of her. Her reading would surely be memorable indeed. We all craned forward, eager to hear what Bettina would say. Yet, to my surprise, Bettina quickly pushed her hand away and made a pleasant excuse about having run out of time and needing to dash. She hurried off.

The woman laughed ruefully and accepted she was too late, but I was puzzled. I'd never seen Bettina react like that before. I made no comment, yet the incident jarred. Time was tight, admittedly, but that didn't normally worry Bettina. On the other hand, it was only a trivial thing. So I took the excuse at face value and quickly forgot it. Bettina certainly never mentioned it again, so no doubt she forgot about it too.

It was only several years later, long after I'd finished working with Bettina – when that same woman suffered a series of unusual and completely unforeseeable tragic events – that the incident came back to me. Could it be that from just that nano-second glance at her palm, Bettina had glimpsed sadness ahead – and didn't want to reveal it? We'll never know now.

At other times, clients occasionally got rather more information than they bargained for – just like my colleague with the two secret girlfriends – and they weren't always pleased.

One day, a distant acquaintance of one of Bettina's business clients decided his wife might be amused if Bettina came to entertain her and her friends with readings, while he and his associates had a day out playing golf.

This sounded like an interesting case for the business book, so we took a taxi from Bettina's home in Highbury to the address on the South London/Kent borders she'd been given. We found ourselves in a leafy street of solid, prosperous-looking detached homes probably built around the 1920s.

The house we were heading for had a large, Tudor-style front door which was opened almost immediately by a tiny blonde woman who could have been Barbara Windsor's younger sister. 'Come in! Come in!' she welcomed us in a wonderful Barbara Windsor voice. 'Can't wait to see what you've got to say!'

She was warm and friendly with a kind, open face, and we liked her immediately. Yet, somehow, she didn't seem quite at ease in her surroundings.

She led us quickly through a square, oak-panelled hall where solemn oil paintings glared gloomily down at us from the stairs. You got the feeling that none of the dour faces in those portraits had any connection with the family that lived here now.

On we went through a spacious kitchen, all luxury units and gleaming granite worktops, and then out into a huge conservatory that ran the width of the house.

Here, at last, our little Barbara Windsor lookalike seemed to relax. This was where the family plainly spent all their time. Bright and sunny, it was filled with potted palms, modern sofas and armchairs, a full-size dining table, and a vast TV. And sprawled contentedly around were Barbara's friends – half a dozen or so sleek women with enviable manicures, designer clothes, and voices straight out of East Enders.

Barbara bustled about fetching tea and sandwiches, and then the running order was established. Bettina was settled in a separate room – another spooky, oak-panelled job with mahogany dining suite and heavy velvet curtains – closed, presumably to protect the furniture from the light. In fact, it was so dark in there that Bettina had to request a lamp in order to be able to see the palms at all.

One by one, Barbara and her friends went to consult Bettina in her dim lair, then returned 20 minutes or so later to the group in the conservatory to compare notes. They all seemed to be amazed and delighted with their readings. All, that is, until we got to the second-to-last woman, a hard-faced individual with drawn-back blonde hair and long tangerine nails.

After a while, she emerged from the dining room looking furious, and the light-hearted chat immediately stopped.

'What did she say?' asked one of the friends.

'It's a load of rubbish,' she said, throwing herself into a chair and lighting up a cigarette.

'Well, she must have said something,' said one of the others.

'It was all wrong. Complete waste of time.'

'That's odd because mine was so good,' said another.

The woman just puffed away angrily. 'Total waste of time. Rubbish.' And she looked so annoyed, no one else dared press her further.

Just then, the front door opened. We heard male voices in the hall and, a couple of minutes later, the husbands appeared in the conservatory. For a group of businessmen, they were all unusually tall with very broad shoulders, faces like granite, and ultra close-cropped haircuts.

'What's the matter, babe?' asked one coming to sit beside the aggrieved blonde. He was dressed in immaculate designer sportswear that appeared to be brand new.

'It was a total con,' she told him. 'So disappointing. Complete rubbish.'

He did not look amused. In fact, I began to feel uneasy. Was it my imagination or was there something slightly threatening about him? I glanced around at the other 'business associates', so big and so tough-looking and so incongruous, somehow, in their spotless sportswear. There was not a golf club to be seen.

The oddest thought struck me. 'They're a load of gangsters!'

At that moment, Bettina's last client emerged, closely followed by Bettina herself.

'Well, must dash. Thank you all for a lovely afternoon,' said Bettina reaching for her coat. She turned to me. 'Come on, let's get out of here!' she whispered. Then – out loud to our hostess – 'So nice to meet you. Do hope you enjoyed it. Thanks again.'

And she hurried me out into the street where, fortunately, a black cab happened to be passing.

'What was all that about?' I asked as we made our escape. 'Why was that woman so annoyed? She said everything you told her was wrong.'

Bettina laughed. 'Everything I told her was right – she just didn't like it.'

'So, what did you tell her?'

'I told her that her man had not long come out of prison, and he would be going back there very soon. She wasn't happy. I don't suppose he will be either.'

On reflection, we decided to leave that case study out of the business book.

CHAPTER 11

While Bettina and I were busy with the business book, the furore over Doris and her money began to die down, and I rather lost touch with the Stokes family.

Yet, behind the scenes, the story was still unfolding. Jane Willis, a pretty blonde former nurse who lived near Southampton, had previously been to see Doris at a couple of her theatre shows. Jane was a natural medium herself. From childhood she'd seen and heard what she now believes were spirit people, and she grew up with an interest in the psychic world. Yet during the 1980s, she was going through a tough time, and she wondered if seeing the famous Doris Stokes in action would be just the morale booster she needed.

'First of all, I won tickets in a magazine competition to see her at the Barbican in London,' recalled Jane. 'It was lovely. Doris was so warm and down to earth, she was like everyone's idea of their ideal grandma. In fact, she even looked like my grandma. At the end of the evening you went out feeling much better than when you went in. I was so impressed that, later, when I heard she was coming to Portsmouth, not far from where I lived, I booked to see her again.'

Jane had recently gone through a divorce and was working harder than ever now; she had to cope with bringing up a family as a single mum. A relaxing evening amongst friendly faces would cheer her up no end she felt. It might even inspire her.

'I was sitting near the front so Doris could see me quite well from the stage,' said Jane. 'Anyway, she came to the edge of the stage, looked down, straight at me and said 'You're a medium too, luvvie, aren't you?' I was a bit embarrassed, so I didn't say anything, but she went on to mention my grandma – who'd been really close to me as I grew up – and also the name Peppy. I had a poodle called Peppy. Then, before she moved on, she said, 'Your grandma's saying don't worry, you'll be alright luv."

Okay, so perhaps it was a very general message, but at the time Jane was fretting greatly over a number of particular issues. She took this to mean that her grandmother knew about her current difficulties and was reassuring her. 'I found it very comforting,' said Jane.

Some months later, on March 6 1987, Jane went to her local spiritualist church as she often did and found herself listening to a young medium called Craig Hamilton-Parker. She had no idea of the significance of the date or of the prediction Doris made to Craig all those years before. She didn't know Craig and had no idea he'd previously met Doris.

'I hadn't heard of him,' said Jane, 'but he seemed to be very good. He gave a lot of evidence to other people, and then, though I was right at the back of the hall, he came to me. He said he was speaking to my grandma and gave her name and a lot of other details – all correct. Then he said my grandmother was telling him he ought to come to me for a reading. This wasn't too surprising to me because although mediums can get messages for other people, they can't usually get messages for themselves. If they want their own reading, they have to go to another medium. So it didn't seem odd – except, of course, for the fact that at that point, Craig hadn't known I was a medium too.'

Could it be that crafty Craig just wanted to see Jane again? Or was Jane's grandma engineering a romance from beyond the grave? Who knows? However it came about, Jane found herself staying behind at the end of the session in case Craig wanted to make an appointment. And, of course, he did.

Having recently come out of one unhappy marriage, a new relationship was the last thing on Jane's mind. She was busy enough caring for her children; she was certainly not looking for another partner. As far as she was concerned, the contact was purely a kindness. Yet, she enjoyed chatting to Craig and agreed to give him his reading.

'I was impressed to hear he was a single dad – bringing up his daughter on his own,' said Jane. 'We talked about being lone parents and the experiences we had in common, and he struck me as very kind.' Plus, they had a shared interest in spiritual matters. They began to meet frequently and somehow, as the months passed, Jane found herself slowly drawn into romance.

During this time, the sad news that Doris had unexpectedly passed away was announced. It seemed a shame, but far off on the south coast as they were, and caught up in the excitement of building a loving relationship, the news didn't appear to have much significance on their lives.

'Not long afterwards, a woman at our church became ill with Lupus,' said Jane. 'I was giving her healing, but I began to feel I could do with some extra help. For some reason, out of nowhere, the idea suddenly popped into my head that I should ask John Stokes. I was puzzled at first, and then I remembered I'd read ages ago that Doris' husband John had been a healer. So maybe he was just the person I needed.'

Jane didn't know John but, through the spiritualist network of friends, she managed to send a request to him.

'I wasn't really expecting to hear back from him,' said Jane, 'but to my amazement, not long afterwards, he phoned. He said he'd be happy to help and would come over to work with our 'patient'.'

A few weeks later, John made good his promise. 'He arrived with a family friend, Rev Terry Carter, who'd driven him down.' said Jane. 'John turned out to be such a sweet, gentle man. It was obvious he was a bit lost without Doris, but he wanted to keep busy and be useful. Anyway, he met my sick friend, put his hands on the top of her head to draw the energy down and gave her healing. It was very peaceful. Afterwards, she said she felt better and also that she was honoured to meet him.

'After that, John visited quite often. He seemed to like coming round. He was interested to hear I'd been a nurse in mental health, just like he and Doris had been, so we had quite a lot in common. He'd always ask me to turn the central heating down when he arrived though! I think I liked my house much warmer than he did. And I used to make him hot-pot for dinner. He loved his hot-pot. His mind would wander a little sometimes, but at others, he was wise and a bit cheeky.

'Sometimes, he talked about Doris and tried to give me advice about being a medium. 'She never got anything wrong you know,' he told me. 'And she didn't like man-made rules and regulations and people telling her how she should be doing things. Just keep doing what you know is right, girl, and don't ever change. Many are called, but few are chosen.'

John never pretended to make predictions, but one evening as they sat chatting he suddenly said to Jane: 'Tell you what, girl. I can see you having a big wedding.'

'You can forget that!' I told him,' said Jane. 'Once was quite enough.'

And yet a few months later, Craig proposed. Jane found herself accepting, and when she walked down the aisle of Bitterne Spiritualist Church on April 1st 1988, she was holding the arm of John Stokes who gave her away.

'As a wedding present, John had the ceremony professionally videoed for us so we could watch it over and over,' said Jane. 'He said to us: 'Just love each other and be good to each other, like Doris and I were good to each other. Be happy.''

They were. Craig moved into Jane's sunny home in a quiet street overlooked by acres of ancient woodland. They were content but it wasn't long before they were dreaming of Craig one day giving up his advertising agency, so they could work together as mediums.

At that point, Jane didn't charge for readings and Craig had a conventional job; they knew if he gave it up, finances would be precarious. Yet the money didn't seem to matter. Out of interest, they began visiting other people who'd already taken the plunge and, towards the end of the year, on a blustery winter's day they found themselves sitting in front of a medium in Brighton.

'Almost at once, he said he'd got a woman through for me,' said Jane. Her mind immediately flew to her grandma who seemed to be good at communicating, but this time Jane was in for a surprise. 'She's got grey hair,' went on the medium, 'and she's saying: 'Fancy seeing you here luvvie! Congratulations on the baby.'

'I nearly fell off my chair.' said Jane. 'The greeting was exactly what Doris would have said. But even more amazing, I was, at that point, six weeks pregnant and the only person who knew, was Craig. We hadn't told another soul. It wasn't my grandma who'd come through – it was Doris and she knew about the baby before even our families did!'

Their little daughter was born the following summer, and life became even busier. Then, one night, Jane had a dream that John Stokes wasn't well. They hadn't seen much of him for some time and she woke up feeling worried.

'I had a strong impression he'd gone over to the other side,' said Jane. 'Then I heard Doris' voice: 'He's over here with me luvvie.' she said, 'He's with us now.' and she was jerking her thumb back over her shoulder.'

Jane didn't realise it at the time, but during individual personal readings, Doris had a habit of jerking her thumb backwards to indicate if the person she was talking about was on the other side, or forwards if the person was still living.

'So we phoned London and discovered that John had indeed passed,' said Jane. 'It was such a shame we hadn't been able to see more of him recently. But, to this day, we both feel when we're doing readings that Doris is often close by, helping out when needed.'

At the time, of course, I hadn't met Craig or Jane and was unaware of these developments. Life was going on for me too. Like Jane, I went on to have a baby daughter and became a busy mum. The name Doris Stokes rarely cropped up these days. Indeed, the fuss surrounding her seemed to have faded away, and my attention was fully occupied with the joys of family life. Doris' smiling face still beamed at me from my bookshelf but – beyond a quick dust from time to time – I didn't give her much thought.

Years passed, school days arrived, and after a while I had enough free time to be able to accept a part-time job on NOW magazine. The crazy, celebrity boom of the new millennium had recently begun and NOW, a weekly celebrity magazine run by dynamic, award-winning editor Jane Ennis, had zoomed to the top of the women's weekly market. What's more, its offices were located in the very same building on the South Bank from which I'd begun my journey to meet Doris all those years before.

It was strange going back. The area had changed for the better, the building for the worse, and Cardboard City had vanished altogether. Along the riverbank, a smart new promenade lured visitors to linger and admire the view. Dingy warehouses had been conjured into arty studios and eateries, derelict sites had sprouted stylish new buildings, and there was even a sand-sculptor at work on the tiny crescent of pale beach revealed at low tide.

No need now for a company bus to ferry the staff back to civilisation. Civilisation had come to us! The building though had not aged gracefully. Never a thing of beauty, at least to our uneducated eyes, it had a dusty, unloved air and a sour, concrete odour – particularly on those axe murderer stairs, now even creepier and dimmer than ever. Perhaps the lifts didn't break down quite as often as they did before but to make up for it, the toilets blocked themselves relentlessly, and towards the end of our stay the air conditioning gave up altogether – at least in the NOW offices.

At one point it was so hot I borrowed a thermometer and discovered that, by mid-morning, it was 93 degrees and rising in our open-plan area. What's more, as we were on the sunny side of the building and the windows didn't open, the blinds were left drawn all day in a vain attempt to keep the room cool. So the magazine was produced in a sauna-like gloom and we reckoned that, strictly speaking, the only way to be comfortable was to come to work in swimwear.

Editor Jane did her best, but the news came down from on high that the air con was unfixable. Also, since there was no official statuary upper limit on temperatures in which employees were expected to work, we couldn't down tools, so we'd better make the best of it. To be fair, management did give us a portable air con unit, but it only wheezed away by the wall, puffing out warm gasps – possibly because it was designed to be filled with ice and if there was any ice to be found in the building, they weren't admitting it to us.

As well as writing features, one of my other jobs was to edit the astrology page – a task for which I was ideally suited, it was felt, on account of my work with Doris Stokes.

So astrologer David Wells was summoned in from the south coast where he worked, to say hello. Given the unappealing state of our office, we tended to meet visitors at a coffee shop up the road. No hardship, as we all jumped at any chance to escape into the cool.

I don't know why but, somehow, I'd imagined an astrologer to be small and owlish – from all that poring over complex astrological charts I suppose. Yet the man who wove his way carefully through the tightly-packed tables looked the opposite of bookish. Very tall and broad-shouldered, he moved powerfully along and heads swivelled as he passed. It turned out that David, who was born in Scotland, the son of a miner, had joined the navy at 16 and spent the next ten years at sea. He served in the Falklands and then on the Royal Yacht Britannia where he met the Queen.

'I remember seeing her for the first time when she was walking up the gangway in Australia,' said David. 'So tiny, but so gracious and very charming. Five of us had just returned from the Falklands, and she knew us all.'

Not the usual background for an astrologer, I couldn't help but think. David agreed. In fact, he'd had no ambitions in that direction until a bout of ill health changed his life. Having left the navy, he was in the middle of retraining for the leisure industry when he became dangerously ill with pneumonia and was admitted to hospital. He doesn't remember much about it until, one night, he seemed to wake up to discover he was no longer in his hospital bed or even in the ward. What's more, still dressed in his pyjamas, he was on his feet and walking.

'I found myself walking down the hospital corridor,' he recalled, 'though I had no idea how I got there. Then, after a while, an old lady appeared and came up to me. 'It's not your time!' she said. 'Go back to bed!' And the next thing I knew, I was back in bed, but somehow looking down at myself lying there.'

That was the turning point in his illness and, from that moment on, David began a slow recovery back to health. Yet, by the time he was well enough to go home, his world seemed to have changed.

His previously calm, unremarkable flat appeared to have taken on a strange life of its own. There were odd noises at all times of the day and night when there was no one around. He heard disembodied voices and sometimes caught a glimpse of shadowy people flitting across the room out the corner of his eye. Once, he could have sworn an unseen figure even lay down on the bed beside him. He could feel the weight of a body press down on the mattress by his side, yet there was no one to be seen.

Not surprisingly, David found it difficult to sleep. Who wouldn't? Was he hallucinating? Could this be some peculiar after-effect of his illness, he wondered, or something more spooky? Could the flat suddenly have become haunted in his absence?

After a few weeks of disturbed nights and worrying days, David looked so tired and drawn, a concerned friend put him in touch with an expert in all things psychic.

She reassured him he wasn't going crazy. She reckoned that David's brush with death had unlocked latent psychic powers he'd never suspected he possessed, and he'd been sent back to the land of the living to use them. 'She became my mentor,' said David. Under her guidance, David began to learn how to cope with the unseen presences that passed through his home. He also began to develop his unexpected new talent. He was told he was well suited to astrology and that studying the stars would be a good starting point. So, there and then, David gave up his plans for the leisure industry and turned to the planets instead.

By the time I met him, David was already an accomplished astrologer and slightly reluctant medium. He was also surprisingly unassuming. Despite being witty, with a wry sense of humour, he seemed uninterested in pushing himself into the limelight.

Yet, of course, when word got out that our NOW astrologer was also a sort of ghostbuster, a number of colleagues with troublesome homes were keen to put him to the test.

First up was Neal, a big, ebullient artist always ready with a joke and an irreverent comment. Neal was always up for a swift pint at lunchtime to celebrate a birthday, a holiday, or any other occasion just crying out to be marked at NOW Towers. Neal appeared to be the typical down-to-earth type – not the sort to be bothered by eerie imaginings in the night, or even to notice them.

Yet there was something unusual going on in his flat he hinted, a touch sheepishly – though he wouldn't be drawn on exactly what.

He was much too busy with pressing magazine deadlines to accompany David on this ghost-busting lark he said, so he handed me his address and his door key and let us get on with it. Us, because I was going along too, to assist if needed, and also write up a feature if anything interesting occurred.

Neal lived on the ground floor of a handsome Victorian terraced house in Battersea. A narrow hall ran from front to back and the rooms that led off it were not large. Neal had filled them with books and artwork and solid, comfortable furniture. There was not a scatter-cushion or girly pot plant in sight – Neal wasn't the frilly type. The whole effect was masculine, lived-in, and not remotely spooky.

Disappointingly, David didn't seem particularly impressed by the rooms. He stood briefly in the centre of each for a moment or two, like a hound scenting the air, but didn't linger. Instead, he seemed drawn to the back of the house and didn't stop until he came to the window right at the end that overlooked the rear garden. Once perhaps a long, grassy idyll where Victorian ladies took tea on the lawn, it was now just a paved yard overshadowed by surrounding buildings. Unfortunately, we didn't have a key for the back door, so we couldn't go outside.

David looked troubled. 'There was a pond down there,' he said peering out through the glass. 'I feel there was water out there and she drowned.'

He turned suddenly from the window, hurried straight back through the room, scarcely glancing at it, and out into the hall. I caught up with him standing at the foot of the stairs, looking up towards the landing above.

'It's a little girl,' said David. 'I think her room was up there on the floor above. She used to come up and down these stairs all the time to get to the garden. There's no bad atmosphere here. She means no harm. I get the impression she's mischievous and playful – running up and down the stairs and rolling a ball around, but she's not a problem. She comes back to play.'

That seemed to be it, so I scribbled the details down in my notebook, and we made our way back to the office. There, Neal admitted that the figure of a little girl had been seen on the stairs and he often heard footsteps, childish laughter, and other unexplained sounds when there was no one else at home. As for a pond in years gone by, he couldn't say, and there was no way of knowing. But it was possible.

Intriguing.

Next was assistant editor Keith. He lived in a very old house he explained, and his children had become inexplicably restless during the night and no longer slept well. Given the age of the property, if there were such things as ghosts, his home would surely be the perfect place to find them.

It turned out that Keith's house was a beautiful, black and white timbered building, possibly Tudor, standing in its own grounds just within commuting distance of London. David and I made our way across fine green lawns, dotted with shrubs, to the oak door. It had recently rained, and a sudden burst of sun set tiny droplets clinging to the leaves sparkling all around us.

Inside, the house was just as attractive. There were massive oak beams, venerable inglenook fireplaces, and an impressive modern kitchen.

'We're told, centuries ago, this was the home of a famous judge,' Keith told us.

Yet David didn't seem to feel the judge was still hanging around. He stared meaningfully at one particular fireplace. 'I think there's a male presence occasionally around there,' he said waving an arm towards the hearth and the handsome fireside chairs, 'but he's not the one causing the problems. Can we see the children's bedrooms?'

So we were led upstairs. David moved back and forth between several smaller rooms and one chamber – with a higher ceiling towards the end of the building – caught his eye. Up at the top of the wall was a small window – surely way too high for anyone to look out of.

'Hmm,' said David rather preoccupied. He was squinting up towards the ceiling. Then, 'Let's go outside again for a minute.'

So down we went, and I followed David around the exterior of the building – no idea what we were looking for. He paced up and down, back and forth until at last he seemed satisfied.

'It's a young man – a servant in those days,' he said. 'Something happened out here a long, long time ago. A terrible accident. Someone was killed – possibly a child. And this young man feels responsible. He felt it was his fault. I don't know whether it was, or not, but he blamed himself, and he was sure he'd get the blame. So he came back into the house and he hanged himself up in that room. But now he can't leave.'

'Why not?' I asked.

'He's afraid,' said David. 'He committed suicide and, in those days, they believed suicide was a sin. He's too scared to move on because he thinks he'll go to hell.'

'So what can you do?' I asked.

'I'll try to persuade him to go to the light,' said David. 'His loved ones will come for him. They'll take him where he needs to go.'

Back we went to the high ceilinged room, and David took up a position in the centre, concentrating hard, trying to get the young man back to talk to him. After a minute or two, it seemed he succeeded. Then, apparently, a silent struggle began. David stood there, inwardly trying to persuade the young man that he wasn't going to hell. He told him if he looked carefully, he'd see a bright light and all he had to do was walk towards it. He'd see people he recognised. People who were waiting to welcome him and all he had to do was go to them.

As usual, I saw nothing, heard nothing, the hair on the back of my neck stayed resolutely flat, and my spine was unshivered. Minutes passed. Birdsong drifted through the little window, then a shaft of sunshine spilling over the floor.

Then all at once, the tension went out of David. He relaxed, gave a sigh and turned to me.

'He's gone,' he said in relief. 'His people came, he could see them, and he went with them.'

Thank goodness for that. The room looked just the same as it did before. Yet, perhaps it was my imagination, but it felt emptier somehow. Lighter. Maybe the tormented spirit really had finally left the building.

David, for one, was satisfied his work was complete. There were probably other old ghosts pottering around the place he felt, but they were inoffensively going about their business, causing no trouble, and he wasn't about to stir them up now.

Over the next few weeks, Keith reported a calmer atmosphere at the children's bedtime. The bedrooms were peaceful and the children seemed to be sleeping better. Once again, there was no way of knowing if it was a coincidence or not. We could only hope David had done the trick.

But word of David's skills was spreading. Around this time, he was also asked to do a guest stint on the popular paranormal TV show, Most Haunted.

Every week, the Most Haunted team, led by presenter Yvette Fielding, spent the night at a spooky location, usually in darkness and attempted to communicate with, and record, any ghosts and ghostly goings-on they encountered.

At this point in the series, controversial medium Derek Acorah was on hand to summon up any lurking spirits in the chosen location and for some reason, when the producers arranged an investigation of a reputedly haunted brewery in Middleton, Manchester, they asked David to join him.

This exciting development for our NOW astrologer should be marked by a mention in the magazine, it was felt. So, before David's first appearance on the show, we had a get-together with Yvette and her husband Karl Beattie. I found the three of them – Yvette, Karl, and David – gathered around the fire in the lounge of a stylish hotel not far from the office.

Yvette, already famous for having been the youngest-ever Blue Peter presenter, and who was to go on to become known as The First Lady of the Paranormal, was petite with reddish-gold hair and wide eyes. Husband Karl was her exact opposite – tall and broad with exuberant dark locks. Legend has it they met on the set of the BBC medical documentary City Hospital where Yvette was presenting and Karl was a cameraman, and Karl proposed live on air. Fortunately Yvette said 'Yes.'

A whirlwind romance it might have been, but they were clearly still happy.

'These two are the most loved-up couple I know,' said David as he introduced them.

Yvette had always been interested in the paranormal she explained, ever since the time, as a child, she saw the ghost of a soldier in her bedroom. Then, years later, when she and Karl had moved into an old farmhouse that seemed to be haunted, they had a sudden brainwave. A live ghost hunt featuring modern technology and scientific investigation could make compulsive TV viewing. So they set up a production company, raided their savings, and Most Haunted was born.

They quickly found a devoted audience but, like Doris, they soon encountered the critics.

'When we get to our location, if nothing happens we're stuffed,' said Yvette. 'But if something happens, they say it's faked. The sceptics will never believe, no matter what you do.'

Nevertheless, undaunted, they battled on, often scaring themselves silly in the process.

By all accounts, the episode which resulted was voted one of the scariest ever, by Most Haunted fans, and David went on to become a regular part of the show.

A brewery seems an odd place to find an apparition, but Greengate Brewery appeared to have been infested with dozens of them.

It all began back in 1828, when a wealthy cotton manufacturer named John Lees bought Greengate House and a row of sixteenth-century cottages on a plot of land in Middleton and, despite no previous experience, decided to build a brewery on the site. The venture prospered. In fact, the business is apparently still owned by the same family and continues to produce fine beer to this day.

Yet the old red brick Victorian buildings, linked by a striking green metal arch over the entrance on which the words Greengate Brewery are picked out in gold, can sometimes take on a sinister air.

Staff report hearing footsteps, bangs and crashes, and heavy items being moved about when there's no one there. A spectral woman has been seen sitting at a table in the boardroom, her face averted; a figure in a long white coat drifts about but disappears when challenged; a tall, dark man has been seen walking towards a set of shelves, then vanishes; and one night, a security guard was slapped hard around the face by an invisible hand when he ventured into the boardroom during his shift.

'I know that's true,' said Becky Keane, a mum and childcare practitioner with an interest in the paranormal, who lives nearby, 'because my husband was a manager with the firm that provided the security for Greengate at the time. It was a good contract, but they began having problems with a high turnover of security guards at the site. Several guards who were posted there refused to go back; in fact, they said they wouldn't enter the premises ever again. Then, one night, my husband found one of his guards waiting outside the building, absolutely terrified. He wouldn't go back in. He said he'd been doing his rounds, checking the boardroom when an invisible hand slapped him round the face – yet the room was completely empty. The poor man ran.'

Researchers discovered that during the original construction, many workers lost their lives while sinking the brewery's well. Over the years, others died by falling into the huge vats and drowning in beer, and in the 1930s a supervisor apparently went missing for days and was eventually found curled up at the bottom of a well – dead.

By the sound of it, there could be any number of seriously displeased former workers with good reason to come back and haunt the place. Greengate was clearly a worthy challenge for Yvette's TV team.

During the night they spent there, Most Haunted recorded all manner of unexplained noises and strange events in the empty building. Large metal barrels were seen to spontaneously shift from their positions and roll across the floor, and David felt himself poked in the back by an unseen hand. He also heard a voice telling him the name 'Thomas'.

Interestingly, researchers later discovered that a weaver called Thomas Hilton once lived at the old cottages bought by John Lees all those years ago.

Yet, though the TV crew seemed to confirm Greengate Brewery was indeed haunted, they don't appear to have put a stop to the unusual goings-on.

In August 2014, yet another tragedy occurred on the site.

One day, a beer tanker pulled into the brewery yard – a common enough sight, of course, but by mid-afternoon, Greengate staff realised they could no longer see the delivery driver. In fact, they hadn't seen him for a while.

He was nowhere to be found in the brewery building or round about, so in the end, someone clambered on top of the vehicle to take a look inside the empty tank. Through the trap door, they spied the missing driver. He was lying motionless below them, right at the bottom of the tank.

Whether he'd gone onto the tanker roof and accidentally fallen in, or climbed down inside to check something and then collapsed, no one could say. It took a dozen fire-fighters to get him out. He was rushed to hospital but, sadly, pronounced dead.

In March 2019, Greengate was in the news again – though thankfully not due to a tragic death. One chilly spring day, passers-by were amazed to see clouds of beer shooting out of the upper storeys of the old brewery buildings, raining down on the street outside and then flowing away across the road in a great amber river.

Apparently, for some reason a tank at the top of the building had overflowed, a spokesman told the press later, and beer had escaped onto the street. There was no harm done and no one was hurt.

Good news, of course. But odd. Distinctly odd.

CHAPTER 12

It was a strange object. Big and bloated like a giant, misshapen football or some sort of unappetising, outsize apple, or maybe even a monstrous tooth; it squatted at the end of a long, dimly lit underpass, all 14 tons of it. A dark, vaguely sinister, man-size silhouette against the bright daylight of the exit behind.

Up close, you could see it was actually made of pale, polished granite, and the entire surface was covered in writing. Ribbon upon ribbon of black gothic script wound round and round the monolith from top to bottom.

So this was the famous 'cursing stone' – source of the 'Curse of Carlisle' recently revived, it was said, after 500 years.

David Wells eyed it apprehensively. 'I'd say this is the worst place to put it,' he said, eyeing the low ceiling and the enclosed space. He stood well back. 'If you thought it was a good idea to display it at all, that is.'

Certainly, Carlisle's latest tourist attraction had been producing a great deal of attention in the press recently – not all of it welcome.

It was an odd story. Apparently, centuries ago, the town of Carlisle in the north of England close to the border with Scotland had been plagued by bands of lawless raiders who plundered Carlisle and villages both sides of the border. They seized sheep, cattle, and anything else they could make off with.

They were known as the Reivers and were comprised of a number of extended family groups who feared neither church nor state. Over several centuries, they became a serious problem in the area, and no-one seemed able to stop their mayhem. Finally, in 1525, the Archbishop of

Glasgow, Gavin Dunbar, exasperated beyond endurance, ex-communicated the Reivers and put a blood-curdling curse on them all for good measure. He ordered his terrifying, thousand-word curse to be read out from every pulpit in the diocese.

'I curse their heads and all the hairs of their heads,' he began. 'I curse their faces, their brains, their mouths, their noses, their tongues, their teeth...' on and on he went... 'from the top of their heads to the soles of their feet...'

And that was not all: 'I curse their wives, their bairns, their servants, their cattle, their wool, their sheep...' and he continued to curse the rest of their livestock, their homes, their barns, their descendants, and everything else he could think of including their cabbage patches. 'May all the plagues that fell upon the Pharaoh and his people of Egypt, their lands, crops and cattle, fall upon them, their equipment, their places, their lands, their crops and livestock...' he raged. 'May the thunder and lightning which rained down upon Sodom and Gomorrah rain down upon them. May the waters of the Tweed and other waters they use, drown them... and I condemn them perpetually to the pit of hell to remain with Lucifer and all his fallows...'

It was possibly the longest, most comprehensive, most hair-raising curse in the history of cursing.

Yet, the Reivers by all accounts were unimpressed. They just shrugged their shoulders and carried on reiving. It was to take another century before they were finally brought under control.

But, of course, that was all a very, very long time ago and by the year 2000 all but forgotten in modern-day Carlisle. What possible relevance could a 500-year-old blast of bad temper have in our brand new 21st century?

None at all it seemed, and the ancient curse would probably have stayed forgotten had it not been for the decision of the city to mark the Millennium with a special gallery, in an underpass, linking Carlisle's 900 year old castle with the city's Tullie House museum across the road. The underpass, which ran beneath the busy A595 dual carriageway, was to contain displays relating to Carlisle's history including a 'Reiver pavement': a black granite pathway boldly inscribed with the names of all the Reiver families – descendants of whom still lived in the city – curving for 80 metres through the passage right up to and swirling around, the foot of a huge boulder carved with the words of the Bishop's colourful curse.

On paper it probably didn't seem a particularly controversial idea. Quite a neat, visual effect, in fact. A sculptor was commissioned, the artwork was completed, and the stone finally installed in 2001. The underpass opened to the public that summer.

Yet, in February that year, presumably even as the construction work was going on, a catastrophic outbreak of Foot and Mouth disease struck the country, affecting the area around Carlisle particularly badly.

Between February and September 2001, around 6 million sheep, cattle, and pigs in Britain were slaughtered in an effort to contain the disease, and a disused airfield at Great Orton just outside Carlisle was used to incinerate and bury hundreds of thousands of the carcasses.

Horrifying pictures of vast piles of burning corpses beneath clouds of black smoke were beamed around the world, with devastating consequences for the tourist trade, to say nothing of the effect on the poor farmers.

It was a terrible time. Yet as autumn set in, the situation seemed to quieten down. Then, in 2004, Carlisle United football team suffered a run of bad luck which culminated in the team being relegated from the Football League for the first time since 1928.

A few months later, in January 2005, the River Eden burst its banks and a terrible flood engulfed Carlisle. Part of the city was cut off for a while, and it was said that 2,700 homes were affected. Three people died and the damage was estimated to cost possibly £400 million.

Around six weeks after that, in mid-February, before the city had even dried out the floodwaters, a huge fire engulfed Rathbones, a prominent local bakery. Seventy firefighters from 14 fire crews fought the flames all night, but the damage was so great the company never recovered and ended up going into administration. Eighty-two people were made redundant.

The following month, in March, one of Carlisle's largest employers Cavaghan & Gray which made ready-meals for supermarkets, announced it was transferring production from its London Road site to Nottingham and closing the factory after nearly 100 years. Six hundred and sixty workers were to lose their jobs.

The people of Carlisle must have looked on aghast. If you wanted to get Biblical, it could appear as if fire, flood, and pestilence had been visited on the city, though not necessarily in that order. What on earth was going on?

Few would disagree the city seemed to be experiencing more than its fair share of misfortune, and a growing number of citizens began to wonder if the bad luck might be caused by the Bishop's stone. Could the resurrecting of that chilling curse have somehow reactivated it and brought disaster down on the descendants of the Reivers who still lived in Carlisle?

A campaign to remove the stone sprang up. Christian groups got involved, and a local Lib Dem councillor asked the council to consider either relocating the stone or destroying it. The press, of course, loved the story.

'I wonder,' said NOW editor Jane, glancing at yet another over-excited headline in the pile of newspapers spread out across the table at our morning meeting, 'I wonder if our David could remove this curse? After all, he's got rid of a few of our ghosts.'

I wasn't sure if an ancient curse was in quite the same league. Neither was David, but amenable as ever, he was willing to give it a try. So, a few days later, we were dispatched north, on a scarlet and silver Virgin train, in an attempt to save Carlisle.

A few hours later, we stepped out onto a busy platform under a vaulted glass canopy. All looked normal. People were bustling about their usual business with no outward signs of panic. Nothing appeared scorched or water-damaged. I seem to recall hanging baskets and food stalls and newspaper stands – all in reassuringly good repair. Trains chugged in and out, announcements echoed and bounced under the glass roof. Shafts of weak sunlight slid through. If there was an air of doom hanging over the station, I couldn't detect it.

Undeterred, we made for the taxi rank and took a quick ride to the subway. Across the dual carriageway we could see the dramatic, red sandstone bulk of the castle fringed by a strip of green lawn. This was the most besieged castle in Britain it was said. A place where once, in a heatwave, prisoners were reduced to licking the damp walls of their dungeons to prevent themselves dying of thirst. But this was no time for sight-seeing we realised. David had a city to save.

Down we went into the subway. At once, the atmosphere changed. We found ourselves in a low-ceilinged tunnel. On one side, the wall appeared to be made of glass tiles, on the other, historical artefacts and information boards were displayed, but what really drew the eye was the floor. Name after name in big, bold capitals was deeply carved into the stone and you couldn't help reading them as you walked.

Carmichael, Batey, Young, Hunter, Jamieson, Gray, Routledge, Bell, on and on they went; so many Reiver families under your feet. It was hard to avoid walking on them. Then, gradually, the tunnel curved and round the bend the big, gleaming blob that was the cursing stone stopped us in our tracks. Welcome daylight from the end of the tunnel beckoned behind it, and it would have been nice to get out into the fresh air – but, of course, that wasn't an option yet.

Unexpectedly, the stone was not alone. Another journalist was already there with a photographer in tow. Oddly, she was striking tactile poses – lying across the granite surface one minute, putting her arms around it the next, leaning against it from one side then the other as the photographer clicked away. She seemed to be enjoying the fun.

David and I exchanged glances. Clearly not the superstitious type, we reckoned, or she might have thought this behaviour unwise. Quite a few locals had been quoted as saying they wouldn't even touch the sculpture, let alone drape themselves over it.

We stood back politely and waited for the pair to complete their work, David assessing the situation the whole time. At last, they finished.

'It's all yours,' said the photographer packing his camera away and they gave us a merry wave as they disappeared into the daylight.

The tunnel was quiet again. David walked slowly around the stone from a respectful distance, examining the curling words. I moved a little closer so that I could get a proper look at the black writing that wound around and around, right down to the ground.

'What d'you think, David?' I asked.

David shook his head. 'I don't know what they were thinking,' he said. 'Putting this curse under the ground strengthens its power. And to read the words, you have to walk around the stone anti-clockwise. That's the way some people believe witches cast a spell. The more people walk round and round this stone, reading the words counter-clockwise, the stronger the 'spell' becomes.'

If that was right, no wonder Carlisle was experiencing problems.

'Can you do anything?'

'I'll try.'

I knew, by now, that David's work wasn't flashy. He tended to keep still and quiet, doing all his communing in his head. So I waited while he moved back towards the wall and directed his gaze towards each 'corner' of the chamber in turn. He was concentrating deeply.

I busied myself, making a few notes. I walked back up the tunnel looking at the names, then wandered down again, past the stone and out of the subway to look at the great castle, now so much closer, at the end of a short path through the lawns. Behind me, traffic raced past on the dual carriageway.

Finally, David was finished.

'What did you do?' I asked as he moved out from the wall and came to look at the castle.

'I've put protection all around the stone,' he said. 'And an angel to stand guard at each corner, so hopefully that will stop any bad influences getting out.'

I glanced back at the stone. Nothing seemed to have changed. Had David lifted the curse of Carlisle and saved the city? Could it be the atmosphere in the tunnel was a little brighter? Very difficult to say. Only time would tell – and time to spare was exactly what we short of now. We had day return tickets, and if we didn't get to the station for the right London train, we'd have to pay a surcharge, which wouldn't go down well with the magazine. We ran.

As far as I know, nothing dramatic happened in Carlisle that night or even that week. But I believe, in the following months, the football team's place in the league was restored, Cavaghan & Gray got more orders and were able to take on more workers, and a new buyer was found for Rathbones.

No doubt Carlisle has had its ups and downs ever since, but perhaps nothing of Biblical proportions. And maybe things did improve after that traumatic time that began in 2001.

So was it down to David, or the efforts and prayers of other concerned well-wishers? There's no way of knowing, of course. But I like to think it was David.

CHAPTER 13

It wasn't the most glamorous of locations – a budget hotel on the edge of Stansted Airport on a cold winter's night. To make matters worse, there was no sign of my interviewees.

'Come around 8pm,' I'd been told. Well, it was long after eight, and there was still not a hint of the people I was supposed to meet. I was on my umpteenth cup of coffee and the brightly-lit charms of the open-plan lounge area – purple I seem to recall or was it aubergine(?) – were beginning to wear thin.

I was here on an unusual mission. I was waiting for the three finalists of a novel new talent show – Britain's Psychic Challenge – to be screened on Channel 5 in the New Year.

A TV company, inspired by a similar show in the Netherlands, had set itself the task of finding the UK's most gifted clairvoyant. Apparently, around 2,000 hopefuls had responded to the appeal, and gradually this army of intuitives had been whittled down to just eight promising contenders. The idea was that these eight would go head-to-head over six weeks, in a series of fiendishly difficult tasks to test their uncanny powers. At the end of each show, the least successful candidate would go home.

Hosted by presenter Trisha Goddard, the show was also to include a team of sceptics who would cast a cynical eye over the proceedings and attempt to suggest various non-psychic ways the competitors could have achieved their results. Any cheating or fakery would be ruthlessly exposed.

'Sounds like an interesting idea,' said Editor Jane back in the office studying the press release we'd been sent. 'I think the readers would like it. Let's go down and talk to the three finalists. We can run the feature just before the final's screened.'

Due to my Doris Stokes connection, I was now more or less the magazine's paranormal correspondent. I was on the case.

Oddly enough, after years of hearing little mention of Doris' name, for some reason tiny reminders were starting to reappear in my life. Turning on the car radio, one day, I was startled to catch the last few lines of a comedy sketch.

'Who d'you think you are?' one character was asking another sarcastically. 'Doris Stokes?'

It gave me quite a jolt. 'Wow!' I thought, 'I haven't heard that name in a while.' In fact, I hadn't heard that name in years. And I was pleased Doris hadn't been forgotten completely.

Then, not long afterwards, on a weekend break to rural Kent, I was walking past the village store in a picture-postcard, half-timbered hamlet when a box of second-hand books on the pavement outside caught my eye. I can never resist books, so I stopped to have a look. As I bent down towards the box, I suddenly found myself face-to-face with Doris. There she was, right on the top, smiling up at me cheerfully from the golden cover of Voices in My Ear. Once again, I felt that jolt of surprise. Doris was on sale for a mere 50p. But, never mind – she was back in circulation!

Over the next few months somehow, when I least expected it, Doris' name would creep into a conversation, and it definitely wasn't me who brought it up. Or a link with her past would appear in an unlikely setting. One afternoon, for instance, after picking up my daughter from school, we popped into a newly-opened gift shop in Bedfordshire so she could spend her pocket money.

This was a serious business requiring a lot of thought, so as my daughter deliberated carefully between the glitter-sparkle unicorns, the cute ceramic puppies, and the multi-coloured crystals, I wandered to the front of the store, browsing the bookshelves as usual. A woman had just walked in and was asking for directions from the assistant behind the counter.

'...No, I don't know the area at all, I'm afraid,' I overheard her say. 'I'm not from round here. I've come up from Wimbledon, today. Wimbledon Spiritualist Church.'

I spun round – that was the church Doris used to visit. The place where she held our book launch party for Voices in My Ear. I was just in time to see the woman thank the assistant and walk out again. It was only a glimpse through the shop window as she hurried away, but she looked very much like the wife of one of the church officials who'd been there on the night of the launch – or at least, the way I imagined she'd probably look now, all these years afterwards. What was she doing here, so far from home, in the middle of nowhere in particular, at the very moment I happened to be here too? There could have been any number of mundane reasons, of course, and there was no way of knowing now, but it felt odd somehow.

Of course, these things were only tiny coincidences. No doubt completely meaningless. But it was strange the way they hadn't occurred before, and now seemed to be coming thick and fast. Having melted almost completely from my attention for so many years, Doris now seemed to be coming back.

Back at the budget hotel, there was a commotion in the lounge. Something was happening at last. The front door opened, gusts of freezing air swirled in, followed by an assortment of well-wrapped but exhausted-looking men and women.

It was nearly 10pm and the TV crew had finally arrived. It turned out they'd just driven down from north Norfolk where'd they'd spent the day filming on Holkham Beach – the vast, three-mile stretch of pale sand and dunes where Gwyneth Paltrow was filmed strolling, in the last scene of Shakespeare in Love.

It was a surprisingly long and tortuous journey from there to Stansted on a dark winter's night, and I wondered why the team hadn't opted to hole up in some cosy hotel near Holkham for the evening.

'Oh we couldn't,' said the production assistant. 'We're flying off to Amsterdam in the morning. First plane. We'll be up about 5am.'

Five am.

It looked like the last thing any of the three psychics would feel like doing after a very long day, was an interview. Fame has its price, I supposed. And despite the pre-dawn start, the next morning, no one seemed likely to get an early night. But I was here to do a job.

Assistants were running around rustling up hot food for the cold and weary team, and I went across to meet my first interviewee.

Diane Lazarus was sitting at a small table waiting for her meal. As I was coming to expect by now, she looked completely normal – more like an attractive businesswoman than the wild-haired, weird-voiced clairvoyant of movie stereotypes. In her thirties, Diane had long, dark hair that curled around her shoulders, friendly brown eyes, and a soft Welsh lilt. She could have been a busy manager stopping off at the hotel for a conference. No one would have guessed she'd spent the day communing with spirits, or whatever it was they'd been up to, on that beach in Norfolk.

I started to open my notebook just as the food arrived.

She was probably starving, but Diane politely ignored the plate in front of her, and patiently spelled out her name for me and told me she came from Swansea. Then she started to explain what a medium did.

'No, don't worry about that,' I said. She looked so tired and her dinner was getting cold. We needed to keep this as short as possible. 'I understand about mediums. I used to work with Doris Stokes.'

Diane looked amazed. 'Really? What did you do?'

'I helped her with her books,' I said.

Diane was even more astonished. 'Years ago, when I was 18,' she explained, 'a psychic told me I'd be the next Doris Stokes.'

And talking to the crew later, I realised that Diane's psychic might have had a point. It turned out the challenge the finalists had been working on that day involved a young boy being hidden in a dip, in miles of sand dunes and marram grass and covered in camouflage netting, so he was more or less invisible.

The local air-sea rescue helicopter and a sniffer dog were then set the task of finding him and their efforts were timed. Next, each of the psychics was sent off in turn to make an attempt. It seemed like an impossible task. There was nothing to be seen in the mile upon mile of featureless dunes.

After many fruitless sweeps, the rescue helicopter had to admit defeat. Two of the psychics also had to give up. Only Diane and the sniffer dog found the boy. Diane apparently walked straight to him, and she was faster than the dog.

'I have to admit I was a sceptic,' the crew member confided, 'but that shook me. It was amazing. I didn't believe in all this stuff, but I know it wasn't faked because it was my son we used out there. Diane genuinely had no idea where he was. There's no way she could have known.'

'So how did you do it, Diane?' I asked.

Diane shrugged. 'I know it sounds mad, but I just saw this great, big arrow, on the horizon above the beach pointing down at a place in the sand dunes, so I walked towards it and kept walking till I found him.'

This wasn't the first time she'd done something like this on the show, it turned out. In one of the earlier episodes, she'd located a soldier concealed under nets and leaves in dense undergrowth in woodland.

These feats were even more impressive when I heard the statistics later. Apparently, Diane found the soldier in seven minutes and the boy on the beach in ten minutes. The sniffer dog took five minutes to find the soldier, but 36 minutes to locate the child. So, Diane wasn't just a little bit quicker than the sniffer dog second time around. She left the hound standing.

Astonishing.

The other two finalists, Mary White from Burnley and Austin Charles, also from Wales, were impressive too. They hadn't managed the beach trial but performed strongly in other types of tests. Both were tucking into their meals when I approached them, but they were very helpful, and by the end of the evening I had more than enough material for the magazine feature.

The story came out as planned and, having met the finalists, I was interested to watch the show. In addition to the beach episode which I already knew about – though I was sworn to secrecy until the show was screened – Diane also seemed to pick up information about a distressing real-life case. Ten years earlier, a pretty Norfolk teenager, 14-year-old schoolgirl Johanna Young, had disappeared from the small market town of Watton, one wintry evening just before Christmas. Her lifeless body was discovered in woodland a few days later. The killer has never been found.

The three psychics were taken separately to the area where Johanna vanished and asked about their impressions. They'd been told nothing about the unsolved murder, we were assured.

Diane walked up and down the narrow country lane. There was nothing much to see. Just a deserted path fringed by trees and hedgerow. It looked quite peaceful and unthreatening – difficult to imagine an act of violence and horror having taken place in such a setting.

After a while, Diane stopped. She said she got an impression of a young girl, a real tomboy who loved drama.

Johanna's mother confirmed this was true of Johanna; in fact, drama had been her best subject at school. Diane paced on and then stopped again – oddly, right at the place Johanna's trainers were found, a voiceover told viewers. Diane mentioned a bike coming up behind the schoolgirl and also that she couldn't see.

It turned out witnesses had mentioned a motorbike being seen in the vicinity, on the night of Johanna's disappearance and also that the weather had been extremely foggy and visibility poor.

Diane was then asked if there was any other important location. She immediately set off straight across the fields towards a small spinney in the distance. On she went for around half a mile until she came to the wood. She scrambled right through the trees and pushed on down a slope until she came to a halt beside a muddy pond.

'She was found here,' said Diane. 'Half in, and half out, of the water and her nose and mouth were full of leaves.'

Once again, this appeared to be correct. The lonely spot was apparently the place where Johanna's body was found.

She'd suffered a fractured skull but the cause of death was actually drowning. The voiceover told us Diane had then gone on to describe the culprit, but her words were not broadcast for legal reasons. The information was passed on to the police. Later reports suggested Diane's description fitted an individual already brought in for questioning but the lead went no further. To date, no one has been charged with the murder, and the case remains unsolved.

All in all, it was an impressive evening for Diane, and I don't think anyone was surprised when she was declared the winner. She left the studio with a gleaming glass trophy and the title of Britain's Best Psychic.

Soon afterwards, as a result of the publicity, Diane was invited to write her autobiography, and she contacted me to ask if I'd help. After all, she'd never forgotten the prediction that one day she'd be the next Doris Stokes. So when, years later, quite unexpectedly, a real live link with Doris – Doris's 'ghost' you could say - turned up to meet her at that Stansted hotel, pen and notebook in hand, it seemed like fate. And perhaps it was, because a few weeks later we got together to work on Mixed Blessings – Diane's gripping story.

Though very different to Doris, like Doris, Diane had a fascinating background. Despite being born and raised in Swansea, welsh as a red dragon, Diane also had exotic links with Africa. It turned out she was descended from Ronald Preston, the great railway engineer who, in 1896, helped construct the Uganda Railway from the coast in Mombasa, Kenya, right across largely uninhabited African bush to Lake Victoria, Uganda. A film was later made about the feat.

In those long-ago Victorian days, a workforce of thousands, mainly recruited from British India where miles of railway had already been built, laid track over 660 miles of wild terrain teaming with big game including man-eating lions.

So difficult was the project, it was later dubbed The Lunatic Line because the route, which involved the logistical nightmare of laying track across rivers, down vast chasms and through areas infested with deadly Tsetse fly, proved highly dangerous and hugely expensive. Hundreds, possibly thousands of workers lost their lives – some mauled to death by lions which dragged them out of their tents at night.

Fortunately, Ronald Preston, along with his wife and baby son reached Port Florence (now Kisumu) on Lake Victoria unscathed. When the railway was finally completed in 1901, Ronald stayed behind and settled in Kenya. Diane never met him, though to this day she has relatives in the area, but later she discovered that as well as being a brilliant engineer, Ronald was also a natural psychic with a keen interest in the supernatural. It looked as if the young Diane inherited his gift down the generations. Like Doris, as a child she saw people no one else could see; as she grew up, she stunned her friends with predictions that came true, and by the time she won Britain's Psychic Challenge she was already something of a celebrity in Wales. She was a regular guest on radio and TV, and her name often cropped up in the local press.

When we met to start work on the book, I drove down to Swansea, and Diane, dressed in vibrant red, took me on a tour. It was a glittering spring day and we started with a brisk walk down the pier looking out over Swansea Bay, crisp blue in the early sunshine with the green hills of the Mumbles in the distance. Then, we drove past the various homes in which Diane had lived, took a look at her old school and the places she used to work, and finally we ended up in the office where she now saw private clients, conveniently situated behind a hairdresser's shop.

There was a cosy waiting room with soft lighting and relaxing armchairs, and hot and cold drinks at hand, but the room where Diane worked was quite plain with a large expanse of bare, white wall facing her desk.

'That's my psychic wall screen!' she said, waving a hand towards the blank space. 'At least that's how I think of it. When a client comes in, I get them to sit to one side so I can see the wall. As I look, pictures of their life appear on the wall. I see what's going to happen.'

So where Doris heard voices, Diane – it seemed – saw pictures.

Yet her work wasn't always office-bound, and she could get results with or without a handy wall, it seemed. She'd done her share of ghost-busting haunted buildings she explained, and she was often asked to try to locate missing people or provide clues in murder mysteries. And there were more unusual requests from time to time.

'Once, a friend who loved history asked if I could pick anything up about the wreck of an old boat that had recently been discovered in Newport,' said Diane.

The boat, now known as the Newport Medieval Ship and reckoned to be a very important historical treasure, had been stumbled upon in 2002 by workers building the town's new Riverfront Arts Centre on the banks of the River Usk in Newport.

One thousand, seven hundred ancient timbers had been lifted from the river bank and taken to a warehouse to be examined by experts. Soon afterwards, Diane was given permission to have a look at them.

If she was expecting to see the skeleton of a ship or anything resembling a vessel when she got there, Diane was to be disappointed. Inside, the warehouse appeared to contain nothing but dozens of yellow plastic baths filled with water. Yet, edging closer, she could make out chunks of venerable wood reclining beneath each surface – not unlike the lengths of driftwood sometimes washed up on the shore at Swansea Bay.

Diane was given a pair of rubber gloves and told that if she was careful, she could dip her hands into the tanks.

'Straight away, when I did, I felt as if I was standing on the deck of a wooden boat,' said Diane. 'I could hear the timbers creaking and see green hills passing by across the water. When I looked down, I noticed the cracks between the planks at my feet were filled with something black that looked like a mix of hair and tar, and there was a boy there. A small boy with blonde curly hair. He was on his hands and knees scrubbing the deck.'

The boy told Diane the boat had been carrying illegal cargoes of silverware and crockery between Newport and Bristol. It had been owned by an Earl who eventually became so greedy, the boy said, he'd had the boat overloaded which caused it to sink. Diane also heard the date, 1426.

'Afterwards, I was told my description of the way the planks had been made water-tight was quite right,' said Diane.

Though the date couldn't be verified – it's now thought the ship may have been built between 1446 and 1466 – she seems to have been correct about the Earl. The experts reckon the ship was probably owned by the Earl of Warwick, a man notorious for paying pirates to capture vessels and booty for him. In fact, it's thought the ship may have been seized from the Portuguese and brought back to Wales for the Earl, where he used it to carry goods between Newport and Bristol.

These days, after years of careful study, the scientists believe the ship had been brought into Newport to undergo some sort of extensive repair, when one of the cradles it was resting on collapsed, tipping the vessel into the soft mud. Presumably, it was either too difficult or too expensive to raise it up again, because it seems to have remained where it fell for the next 500 years.

As talk of Diane's uncanny abilities spread, some people were sceptical, but others fascinated. One, in particular, Peter Hall, a former policeman turned TV cameraman who lived not far from Diane, was keen to see if he could capture her psychic powers on film.

To this end, from time to time, he took Diane to an unknown destination, told her nothing about it and then started filming as she wandered around trying to gain clues as to what could have happened in this spot. One of the resulting films, about a young girl called Muriel Drinkwater, can be seen on YouTube.

'It was a very upsetting case,' Diane recalled when she told me about it. 'In fact, it was so harrowing, I told Peter afterwards, that I never wanted to do anything like that again.'

Muriel's story was long forgotten by most people by the time Peter came across it. Certainly, Diane had never heard of the case. It all happened back in June 1946 – 20 years before Diane was born. One afternoon, a young welsh girl called Muriel Drinkwater, aged 12, stepped off the school bus as she usually did and set off down the narrow country lane that led to her parents' farm a mile away. She was never seen alive again. Somewhere along the path, she disappeared. Her body was found the next day dumped in woodland some distance away. There was a huge manhunt, but her killer was never found.

As usual, Peter said nothing about the case but took Diane to his mystery destination, a remote country lane through deserted woodland. It was a lonely spot where the trees met overhead in a gloomy tunnel.

After moving around a little, absorbing the atmosphere, Diane said she could hear a sweet voice singing. Then she saw a little girl who looked about nine she reckoned. The child told her she was actually twelve and showed Diane a pixie hat, some gloves, and a blue school mac.

Diane was puzzled as she could see leaves on the trees which meant it wasn't winter, so these clothes didn't seem appropriate. The girl told her it had been cold that day and was likely to rain, so she'd worn her winter things.

Diane then described seeing a man approaching. At first, it didn't seem alarming, Diane got the impression Muriel knew him. But then unexpectedly he grabbed her, dragged her into a nearby field, and raped her brutally.

'He stabbed her,' said Diane, horrified. 'But then he pulled out a gun and shot her too. She was stabbed and shot.'

When Peter checked the information with the police later, he discovered Diane had been correct. Even the singing that Diane heard made sense. Apparently, Muriel had such a lovely voice that she was known as the 'little Nightingale' and she often sang to herself as she walked home.

Diane felt the killer was a local man from a farming background who was still alive at that point. But once again no arrests have been made and, after all these years, it looks as if he got away with the crime.

'That case really shook me,' said Diane. 'I felt as if I saw the whole thing and I could do nothing about it. It was awful. That's why I wanted to call my book Mixed Blessings. People often say they think it must be brilliant to be able to do what I do but, you know, sometimes it's not. Sometimes, I don't want to know the things that are going to happen. It can be quite a burden.'

And, on a lighter note, it can be difficult for friends and family too. 'They can't give me a surprise present,' said

Diane. 'I always guess what it is. And I know if someone's lying too. There's really no point in lying to a psychic!'

Bearing in mind it's not always a good thing to know what's going to happen in the future, I didn't ask Diane to do a reading for me. Yet, I did get a tiny taster. When we were finishing the book that summer, I took my daughter along for a visit to Diane at home during the holidays.

Emma was about 16 then, and just waiting for her GCSE results. Diane asked what she wanted to do when she left school.

'I don't really know yet,' said Emma.

Diane glanced away briefly – probably looking at the wall – then looked back.

'You're going to be a teacher.'

Emma shook her head. 'Oh no. That's the last thing I'd want to do,' she said firmly.

Diane smiled. 'I can see you surrounded by children. There are children all around you, and I heard the word 'teach'. You're going to be a teacher.'

Emma was too polite to argue, but the idea didn't please her.

'I don't like children!' she insisted on the way home. 'I'd hate to be a teacher. She's completely wrong.'

A-Levels followed, then university, and Emma considered a number of interesting careers. But then, through a series of unexpected coincidences, she found herself organising a week-long music festival at a local school. To her surprise, she loved it and the head was so impressed with her efforts, she was offered a permanent job.

Today, Emma is a gifted and creative teacher, and the children adore her. She wouldn't want to do anything else.

CHAPTER 14

It was a sumptuous breakfast. Arranged on a side table, towards the back of the pretty cafe/tearoom, was fruit juice, cereal, pots of tea and coffee, big platters of crispy bacon, sausages, eggs, tomatoes, baked beans, fried potatoes, mushrooms, and stacks of hot toast. The perfect full English, in fact, perfectly cooked.

The only problem, as far as I was concerned, was the time. Barely 7.30 in the morning, it was a bit early for me to do the meal justice. Fortunately, the other members of the breakfast club were made of tougher stuff. Admirably bright-eyed and wide-awake, despite the hour, they congregated enthusiastically around the food, piled their plates, then settled down at the communal table to get stuck in. Meanwhile, Toni, the cafe owner, a petite blonde whirlwind of a woman, who also happened to be a club member, cast a professional eye over the food and made sure the toast kept coming.

It was the very end of the recession and my husband, like many others in the construction industry, had suffered a frustrating few years with little work. No amount of local advertising or fliers seemed to make any difference, and he was beginning to think it was time to retrain for a different career.

'Why not join a networking group?' suggested a helpful friend one day.

We'd heard of networking, of course, but doubted there'd be anything so progressive nearby. Well, shame on us for being so negative. A quick Google search turned up the ideal group just a few miles away. Small, friendly, and relaxed, with few rules and a lot of laughter, the Leighton Buzzard Breakfast Club welcomed my husband immediately. Although not a fan of very early starts, I went along too for moral support.

And, amazingly, it worked. Shame on us again for being doubters. It wasn't long before building work began to trickle in and thoughts of retraining and different careers faded away.

Yet, strangely, this particular morning it was me, not my husband, who found a new project.

Over by the food table, Chairman Steve Baker was pouring more juice. 'Ah, Linda – didn't you say you were a writer?' he asked.

'That's right,' I said, helping myself to another cup of black coffee. It was a cold winter's morning, and outside the window I could see it was still dark. Technically, it was morning, but my brain was registering the middle of the night.

Steve didn't appear to notice. Steve was a financial advisor. Always immaculate and always amongst the first to arrive despite living the furthest away, Steve kept us up-to-date with the latest hints and tips on pensions and investments and planning for the future.

'Thought so,' said Steve. 'Well, I don't know if you'd be interested, but I've got this client who's looking for someone to help her write a book. Apparently, there's a publisher all-arranged, but she needs someone to put the words together.'

'Sounds interesting,' I said. 'Any idea what the book's about?'

Steve looked vague. 'Something to do with orbs I think.'

'Orbs?' I said. I couldn't say I knew anything about orbs. A faint memory surfaced. I seemed to recall having read somewhere of mysterious balls of light, invisible to most people, that apparently appeared and disappeared without warning and were often caught on camera. They were known as Orbs, I believed. But how you filled a book about them, I couldn't imagine.

'Yeah, something like that,' said Steve vaguely. It was clearly not his field. 'I don't really know the details, but I'll put you in touch with Peggy. She'll tell you all about it.'

Which is how a few days later, I came to be walking up the steps to Peggy Weber's magical pink cottage on the edge of town.

There really was an other-worldly air about the place.

Completely hidden from the street, tucked away behind a modern housing estate and approached by a cracked concrete drive that appeared to lead only to a row of garages, you rounded the corner to find the path unexpectedly open out onto a wide frontage vibrant with pots of flowers, wind chimes, and cheerful ornaments. Yet, screened as it was on all sides by tall trees and the rear wall of the garage block, it was an invisible, secret plot.

Peggy flung open the door just as I reached the top of the steps. A tiny figure with honey-coloured hair and a beguiling Irish lilt, Peggy fizzed with energy.

Someone once joked she must be part leprechaun and you could see what they meant. Spontaneous and full of fun with a lively sense of humour and wry wit, there was something fey and sprightly about Peggy. Laughing one minute, close to tears the next at news of some fresh act of cruelty somewhere in the world, Peggy couldn't keep still for long.

She'd filled her home with plants and artwork; candles, models of fairy-folk, animals and interesting curios she'd picked up along the way covered every surface. Peggy loved old, well-worn things with plenty of character showing.

'But why orbs?' I asked as we reached the kitchen and she put the kettle on for tea. 'How did you get interested in orbs?'

Peggy took a camera out of her pocket. As I was to learn later, she never went anywhere without it. It was a very small, digital job that fitted easily into one hand; very simple to operate and one of the cheapest on the market.

'Orbs just seem to come out when I take pictures,' she said. 'Let's see…'

And tea forgotten, she was off through the dining-room, camera in hand. 'Bring your book,' she called over her shoulder.

As Peggy didn't know me and was apparently looking for a writer, I'd brought along a copy of Doris' Voices in My Ear to show her as an example of my work.

I hurried after her, paperback in hand.

Through the dining room and down another hall we went until we emerged in Peggy's spacious bedroom. On the wall opposite the bed were three striking pictures of the most important men in Peggy's life – her spirit guide, her beloved late husband Tony, and a print of the famous pre-Raphaelite painting of Jesus, standing outside an overgrown front door, lantern in hand – Light of the World.

An armchair had been positioned beneath Light of the World, and on the chair stood a book.

'I'll just move Harry out the way,' said Peggy, picking up the volume, 'and you can put Doris there.'

I stared at the book in her hand. The black and white photograph on the cover, of an elderly man in a medical coat, looked familiar.

'Harry…' I said. 'That's not Harry Edwards is it?'

'Yes,' said Peggy, surprised, 'how did you know?'

Harry Edwards, once a renowned healer, had been a great friend of Doris. I'd never met him. He'd passed away before I started work with Doris, but she often talked about him. In fact, she credited him with curing her husband John of stomach cancer, and she mentioned him in her books. She'd once shown me a picture of the two of them, and I knew that the healing sanctuary Harry had opened at his former home in Surrey – where Doris visited him –was still operating.

'That's amazing, Peggy,' I said. 'I didn't know there was a book about him. Harry and Doris were friends.'

'Oh, well, in that case,' said Peggy putting the book back, 'they can have a chat,' and she placed Doris' book, emblazoned with Doris' smiling face, on the chair beside it.

It was an intriguing sight – the two old friends, Harry, in his white coat, and Doris, resplendent in pink on a sunny day, reunited on a velvet seat at the foot of Peggy's bed.

But Peggy was busy. Gesturing to me to move to one side so she could properly see her subjects, she began snapping away with her little camera.

'Doris,' she said to Doris' radiant features, 'look who's come to see you! Linda's here.'

Doris made no reply, of course, but that didn't bother Peggy. She carried on clicking until suddenly she seemed satisfied. She turned over the camera to view the screen on the back and began scrolling through the pictures she'd just taken.

'Ahh. There you are. Look at that!' said Peggy, evidently finding what she'd been looking for. She handed me the camera.

There on the screen, was a shot of the chair with the two books stood side by side on the seat, and just above Doris' book was what appeared to be a large translucent soap bubble, shining pink. I'd been staring at the chair and the books the whole time and saw absolutely no sign of any bubble whatsoever – yet there it was, plainly visible on camera.

Next, Peggy got me to sit in the chair and hold the books while she took more pictures. I felt a bit silly, but Peggy didn't care how I looked or how I posed.

Minutes later, there I was, captured on the tiny screen in a series of umpteen near-identical shots, except for the fact that in some of the images there was a blue bubble gleaming above my head and in others, a transparent bubble on my elbow.

These quirky little globes of light were obviously what people meant when they talked of 'orbs'. Yet they were completely invisible to me, even while one was apparently sitting silently and weightlessly, on my arm.

They say the camera doesn't lie – but is this actually true, I wondered.

I looked at Peggy's little camera. It was the plainest, simplest digital affair. In fact, I had a similar one, myself, at home. Only mine had never presented me with anything resembling an orb. Then again, not all of Peggy's pictures contained orbs either. Yet a surprising number did.

So how was this possible? There was no film inside to get damaged, there were no fancy effects to select on the controls and this wasn't a case of doctoring the image on the computer later, because I was viewing the pictures seconds after they were taken, while they were still on the camera screen.

Perhaps there was a complicated technological explanation to account for this, but it was beyond me. I suspected it would have been beyond Peggy too because, as she'd be the first to admit, she was obviously not the technical type. Operating her laptop was quite a struggle and sending an email a major challenge. In fact, machinery of all kinds was difficult for Peggy. I couldn't imagine her having the expertise, or the patience, to be able to manipulate images on a computer.

'So how did all this start?' I asked, when she finally remembered the abandoned kettle and dashed back to the kitchen to finish making tea.

'Well, when my Tony was very ill, but still able to get out,' said Peggy, 'he went off one day and came back with a computer and a digital camera. He said it was a present for me.' Knowing he wouldn't get better it seemed, Tony decided Peggy needed a hobby to distract her in the days ahead. Peggy, however, wasn't too thrilled with the gift.

'I thought he'd gone mad,' said Peggy. 'I couldn't use a computer, and I didn't know anything about photography. And I wasn't interested in taking pictures. It was the craziest present for someone like me. I couldn't imagine why he'd bought it.'

Yet, perhaps, even long before Tony's gift, something was brewing.

As she told me about her life for the book she wanted to write, I realised Peggy had always been a bit unusual. Born in a rural backwater in the republic of Ireland at the end of World War II, Peggy was one of 17 children. With so many mouths to feed, money was in short supply in the household and with no TV, central heating, phone, or any of the luxuries we take for granted today, the children spent most of their free time playing out of doors in the fields, and gathering wild berries, nuts and any other tasty treats they could find to bring home for tea.

In those days, the Catholic Church was the heart of the village. Everyone was expected to attend mass on Sundays – though Peggy's rebel dad refused. The priest was possibly the most important figure in the community, the village school was run by nuns, and organised religion was taken very seriously.

Despite Ireland's reputation at the time as a mystical place, where belief in the 'little people' and enchantments was supposedly widespread, any weird, supernatural talk was deeply discouraged.

So, when a very young Peggy noticed angelic figures, rather like the statues of the saints she saw in church every week, gathered around the top of the local water-tower as they walked home one afternoon, her worried mother shushed her and told her not to mention such things to anyone.

Similarly, when Peggy skipped down to play on the banks of the nearby stream, as she regularly did, she was entranced to see tiny coloured lights come dancing out from the undergrowth and zip around like brilliant butterflies. It seemed to her that they were trying to attract her attention, putting on a wonderful show for her private amusement. She'd watch the miniature ballet for hours and (to herself) she called the display her 'magic lights'. 'Hers' because they only appeared when she was alone. Yet, ever mindful of her mother's disapproval, she never mentioned them to anyone.

As she grew older, Peggy realised she wasn't the only one banned from discussing certain subjects. Peeping through her granny's cottage window one day, she was surprised to see granny and a number of the village mums, gathered around the kitchen table, peering into teacups. It turned out her Romany grandmother – who'd abandoned the open road for love and now lived like everyone else in a settled home – quite often held little get-togethers where she secretly read the tea leaves. But, once again, the unspoken rule was always followed. Not a word of what went on behind granny's tightly-closed front door could filter out, for fear of reaching the priest.

Peggy's education was brief and basic. She left school at 14 and at 16, like many other girls in the village, she was sent to England to work as a cleaner or mother's help. It was a well-trodden career route. The girls received their board and lodgings overseas, which took the pressure off the crowded households back home, and they sent their meagre wages back to boost the family budget.

Peggy didn't intend to stay in England forever of course, but within a few weeks of starting work in a Catholic boarding school, she took a stroll on her afternoon off and came face to face with the boy who was to become the love of her life. Young Tony Weber, still at school himself, lived just up the road from Peggy's new home. It wasn't long before the couple were teenage sweethearts.

They went on to marry and raise four children and Peggy's dreamy, other-worldly ways faded into the background. It was only years later, after Tony sadly passed away, that Peggy's life took an unexpected turn.

She came across the camera one day, now long forgotten and gathering dust in a drawer, and for some reason decided to try it out. Her children, now grown-up, were visiting and Peggy took some shots of her son walking in the garden. But when she came to look at the snaps, she thought there must be a fault on the camera. Quite a few of the pictures looked as if they'd been embellished with baubles off the Christmas tree.

It didn't happen every time. Peggy took more and more photographs to try to see what was causing the problem. Many of them came out fine. Yet, now and then, without warning, one or two 'bubbles' would show up in random places on an image. Occasionally, dozens would appear. It was very puzzling.

After a while, taking pictures became quite compulsive. Peggy couldn't resist trying the camera to see what would happen next. Gradually, a strange idea began to form in her mind. It was almost as if the orbs had an intelligence of their own – that they responded to her. If she called out a request for an orb to appear, then took a photograph, invariably somewhere in the frame, a shining bubble could be seen.

'So, these days, I talk to them,' Peggy explained. 'I don't care if I sound crazy. I call them 'lads' and ask them to come and show themselves, or let me know what they think.'

In fact, Peggy is now quite convinced that orbs are actually the form that spirits of the departed take, so they can be seen in this world. With this in mind, she feels she's able to keep in contact with her beloved Tony.

'He's never far away,' said Peggy. 'If I chat to his picture on the wall and then photograph it, a big pink orb will appear right on the picture. He even helps me make decisions. A while ago, we were decorating my bedroom, and I couldn't choose between several shades of paint. So I painted a stripe of each colour side by side on the wall and asked Tony to show me the one he liked best. Then I photographed the wall. Sure enough, an orb appeared right in the centre of one of the stripes – so that's the colour the room was painted.'

Before she discovered this unique means of communication, Peggy had visited mediums and various spiritualist events in an effort to hear from her man. She'd had quite a few reassuring messages she told me, but also some items that were nothing to do with Tony.

'I saw a psychic artist once,' she said, 'and she did this picture of one of my guides – or possibly me in a past life. I'll show you.'

And she darted off to her bedroom again, rummaged around for some time, and eventually returned with a laminated A4 sheet. She handed it to me.

I stared at it in surprise. I was looking at a portrait of a blue-eyed woman, dressed as a nun in a sky blue habit. It looked oddly familiar. Surely I'd seen her somewhere before? Then it came to me... from years and years ago. That little clay model of my disappointing, not-Cleopatra-guide made for me by Margaret Muntz at Stansted Hall three decades earlier.

'She's a nun,' Margaret had said.

'She's a nun,' Peggy said, coming to look at the picture over my shoulder.

'But why isn't she in black?' I asked.

'A lot of orders wear light blue,' said Peggy. 'It's the colour of the Virgin Mary.'

Hours later, when I was back home, I went in search of the Margaret Muntz model. I hadn't seen it for years so didn't hold out great hopes of finding it. Amazingly – some might say miraculously since my filing system is a disgrace – it quickly turned up, still wrapped in the purple plastic bag in which I'd stored it so long ago. The colours were as fresh and bright as the day Margaret painted them. My little nun's headdress was white but otherwise with her blue eyes and sky blue habit she was very very similar to Peggy's. Odd.

But while still at Peggy's, there wasn't time to mull over the possible coincidence. Peggy had come to a decision. She put away the psychic portrait, and we settled down to discuss the book she wanted to write. It was to be an autobiography called My Magic Lights she said, and she intended to include a batch of her most interesting photographs in the publication. She was quite happy for me to help her. Any friend of Harry's was a good omen, as far as she was concerned, so we arranged to meet the following week to get started.

Still chatting, we walked to the door. It had fallen dark by now. The moon was already high in the sky, and it was a pin-sharp, crystal-clear winter's night. As I walked away, across the forecourt, I turned back to give Peggy a friendly wave. There she was, standing on the doorstep, camera in hand clicking away enthusiastically again.

'Ooh. Look, look!' she called suddenly, and she ran down the steps, full of excitement to show me the pictures.

Like frames of a film, a series of shots of my warmly-wrapped figure walking away from the door unspooled before my eyes. At the beginning of the sequence, I was clearly visible but, gradually, a swirl of white mist appeared at the side of a frame. The next frame showed the mist increasing and, in each succeeding frame, more mist was pouring across the forecourt, streaming closer and closer to me until it looked as if I was walking through thick smoke.

I stared at the little screen in disbelief. There had been not the slightest hint of fog in the air. There was no smoke. Visibility was perfect. It still was. I'd seen no hint of any mist as I walked away and I'd certainly have noticed if I'd found myself wreathed in wispy clouds of white. The camera doesn't lie… so how could this be?

'Must have been the cold,' a logical friend suggested later when I described what happened. 'Something to do with the camera coming out from a warm house into the cold night air. Maybe it was some sort of condensation effect.'

Maybe it was. And I'm sure experts can tell us. But still, it seemed odd.

Over the next few months, I saw many more of Peggy's pictures. She saved her camera cards – dozens and dozens of camera cards – and loaded them onto her laptop so we could view them on a bigger screen. Unfortunately, being the artistic type, Peggy didn't have a reliable filing system so she couldn't always find the shots she wanted to show me. Yet the examples she came across were striking enough. Some of the orbs were extraordinary. They appeared to come in a range of sizes and colours, some almost as big as footballs, some as small as golf balls. No two were quite the same. Some were completely transparent, others more solid, and a few contained misty shapes that could be figures or faces.

Usually, they appeared in ones and twos, but occasionally they arrived in extraordinary multitudes – great battalions of shining orbs filling the sky.

I witnessed this phenomenon once, when we drove down to the seaside town of Felixstowe to visit Peggy's daughter Pat, a talented artist who was designing the cover of My Magic Lights.

That evening, after a day spent playing around with various photographs, backgrounds, and typefaces, Pat took us to her favourite restaurant for dinner.

Once the meal was over, Peggy was itching to get out there onto the sand.

The prospect was not inviting.

A chill wind was blowing salt-laden debris along the gutter and whipping our hair into our eyes. We could hear the waves churning angrily somewhere out in the dark. The promenade was completely deserted, as was the beach.

'Just a couple of shots,' she said, and she was off across the road, camera in hand, and down the steps to the sand before we could stop her.

Pat and I followed, more slowly.

For a moment, on the beach, I couldn't see Peggy at all but as my eyes adjusted to the dark I caught sight of her small figure. She was out near the water's edge, oblivious to the wet sand soaking into her shoes, camera pointing towards the ocean, happily snapping away.

A sliver of moon appeared between the clouds and silvered the incoming waves. Even so, it was very dark. Surely the camera's tiny flash couldn't cope with the gloom?

Yet, after a few minutes, Peggy rushed over, eyes alight, to show us what she'd captured.

Once again, I was astonished. There on the camera's mini-screen was a beautiful seascape – dark waves, silver moon and a sky filled with shining, transparent orbs – hundreds and hundreds of moonlit globes dancing above the waves.

I looked from the camera to the water and the sky.

Nothing.

Just black, billowing clouds edged with silver and a dark, dark, faintly moon-washed sea.

So what had Peggy captured on her camera?

Could it be something to do with water vapour in the air? Or the movement of the waves? Or the energy they generated, somehow picked up and recorded as spheres by the digital mechanism?

I had no idea.

Peggy was quite certain there was a lot more to it than that. Apparently, on visits to her daughter, she and Pat often came down to the beach for an hour or two after dinner to take pictures.

Normally the orbs arrived as soon as Peggy started shooting but on one particular night nothing happened. No matter what she did, Peggy was unable to persuade a single orb to show itself.

It was baffling and disappointing.

Yet, despite the fact the weather was deteriorating rapidly, Peggy was unwilling to give up and go home.

'So we moved further along the coast towards the old town,' said Peggy, 'and tried again and it worked perfectly. The orbs came back good as ever.'

She still couldn't understand why they'd let her down earlier, but at least the evening hadn't been completely wasted. She clicked away with her camera in the teeth of a gale until at last – satisfied with a reasonable haul of orb pictures – they went home.

It was only the next day they realised how lucky they'd been.

Pat opened the local paper to find a dramatic account of storm damage to the promenade and a nearby cafe almost washed away by massive waves – right about the spot where she and Peggy had been standing.

It was almost as if the orbs had led them away to safety.

And Peggy's camera didn't confine itself to orbs. Sometimes it appeared to detect other mysterious shapes invisible to the naked eye.

Peggy explained that wherever she was, she frequently got the feeling she must take a picture – NOW. And mostly she did. People, buildings, landscapes – it was all the same to Peggy.

When inspiration struck, she photographed whatever happened to demand her attention. There were pictures of wheat fields at night where strange strings of dainty lights were captured bright against the dark sky, just above the growing crops.

One afternoon, she'd jumped out of a car to snap an old country church and high on the wall above the door, a small, glowing patch was visible on the camera's screen. Later, when enlarged on her laptop at home, the glowing area revealed itself to be the shape of a tiny, fiery angel. And, in Peggy's back garden at night, her camera frequently recorded mist spiralling in from the hedge, sometimes forming into the likenesses of ghostly, life-size figures.

These days, Peggy was often in her garden after dark. She'd become interested in healing – hence her copy of the Harry Edwards book – and had taken to writing the name of a sick person in chalk on a slate and placing it in the centre of her healing circle on the lawn. Then, she would ask for healing for this individual, stand back, and begin taking photographs.

The result would usually be one or more shining orbs hovering around the slate. Sometimes, there would be white mist too and – once or twice – the mist seemed to wind itself into the suggestion of an angel with folded wings. Peggy took this to mean that healing and love were on their way to the ailing person.

Over the next few months, I grew accustomed to Peggy's compulsive photography. She was particularly keen to visit Harry Edwards' sanctuary at Burrows Lea in Surrey to see if she could learn more about spiritual healing and I was happy to go along.

By this time, I'd learned a few more details about the great man. Apparently, at the height of his fame in the 1950s, he received around 10,000 letters a week and gave public demonstrations of his work to audiences of thousands. He filled the Festival Hall in London, and people came in their hundreds to meet him in person at his sanctuary.

Set in acres of tranquil gardens with wonderful views of the Surrey Hills beyond, Harry's old home turned out to be a substantial Victorian villa with a serene, country house air. Peggy loved it.

In the oak-panelled hall with its inglenook fireplace, she captured numerous orbs lingering around the fireside chairs, while I wandered about wondering what the place had been like when Doris visited and Harry was still living there. Perhaps Doris had walked through this same hall and sat drinking tea in one of those wing-backed chairs? She'd certainly have enjoyed the beautiful gardens.

By the time we left, Peggy was more inspired than ever to continue her healing work. She'd filled her camera card with endless pictures and promised to send a selection back for the slightly bemused sanctuary staff.

In the car, Peggy finally put the camera away and sat back to relax.

It was a funny thing about that camera. You'd think, from the pictures Peggy produced, there must be something special about it. But I'd tried it myself. Once or twice, I'd taken a few snaps with it. They came out ok, but they were completely unremarkable. Not an orb could be seen in any of the pictures.

Yet with Peggy's finger on the button, glowing spheres appeared. And it wasn't just this particular camera. After a while, the old camera began to get battered and worn, so Peggy bought a new one. Another cheap, easy-to-use chain store model. The orbs continued, as before.

Perhaps one of the most touching shots was a tiny little picture Peggy took the following March, on the evening of her wedding anniversary. She showed it to me the next day.

I stared at the image.

Standing just outside the house was the little side table from the sitting-room. Peggy had carried it out into the garden and carefully placed two long-stemmed glasses, and a bottle of chilled white wine, on it.

'So, I said to Tony,' she explained, 'come on babes, it's our anniversary! Have a drink with me to celebrate. Then I poured wine into both glasses and took this picture.

And there, right on the rim of one of the glasses – just where you'd put your lips to sip – was a perfect orb.

That said it all for Peggy.

Tony had come back to toast their big day.

CHAPTER 15

Now where was that letter? Some time ago, quite out of the blue, I'd received a note from a woman who used to live near Doris Stokes' old home in South London. Lyn Gibb-de Swarte, a former editor of Psychic News and a medium herself, wrote to tell me that years before, she'd attended an auction of Doris Stokes memorabilia and come away with quite a number of interesting pieces. It occurred to her that I might like to pop in and see them some time.

I was surprised. I'd heard nothing about an auction, but then it struck me that the sale had probably been advertised locally and taken place several years after Doris passed away – around the time I'd lost touch with the Stokes family.

Intrigued, I phoned the number Lyn sent, and she filled me in on what happened during those lost years. Apparently, in the decade following Doris' death, her alleged 'missing millions' completely failed to turn up (no surprise to me!). Unfortunately, various large tax bills did, and the family had no means to pay.

Sadly, the pride-and-joy semi had to be sold, and in an effort to raise a little more cash, Doris' personal possessions went under the hammer too. Even the little china figure of a balloon-seller that Doris had promised as a keepsake to her agent Jenne Casarotto, was packed off to the auctioneers.

I knew Doris wasn't really bothered by material things. She didn't even care what happened to her remains after she'd gone. 'I'm leaving my body to medical science if they want it,' she used to say jauntily. 'It'll be no good to me. It's just my old overcoat.'

And, in fact, if you asked her about her beloved house, I reckon she'd have said she was glad to think of another family enjoying living there, once she had no further use for it. But, all the same, it seemed a shame to think of everything gone.

The auction had been advertised in Psychic News, Lyn went on, and the event was well attended. She'd gone home with several odds and ends that might be familiar to me, so if I'd like to come over and see them some time, I'd be very welcome.

My mind immediately flew to the replacement for the ceramic Shire horse I'd accidentally broken, when Doris moved home all those years before. It would be good to see that again. To be honest, I couldn't really recall any other items that might have wound up in the sale. It would be interesting to accept Lyn's invitation and see what she'd found. Yet, at that point, there wasn't time. Lyn lived quite a distance away and, as usual, I was racing to meet various difficult deadlines. I couldn't justify a whole day away.

Now, however, it was different. Several years had gone by, Doris was on my mind, and it was a beautiful early autumn day. Perfect for a drive out to the Fens where Lyn now lived with her wife Cathy. 'Of course you can come over,' said Lyn when I contacted her. 'Come and have lunch.'

It was a complicated route that took me past the splendid bulk of Ely Cathedral – the famous Ship of the Fens – and out into the vast skies and deserted, chequerboard fields beyond.

As I drove, I couldn't help thinking about the Wikipedia entry for Doris I'd made the mistake of looking up before I left. This was when I discovered that, as well as claiming Doris was a fake, it also recorded she was once described as 'a ruthless, money-making con artist.'

That really did surprise me. Who could have come to that conclusion I wondered? In ten years of working with Doris, I could truthfully say I never witnessed a single example of ruthless or mean-spirited behaviour.

As for money, the only time Doris mentioned it was when the accountant was complaining about her horrendous phone bill.

When I first met her, Doris' charges were modest in the extreme and later – when she was inundated with requests and prioritised parents who'd lost children – she usually gave her services for free.

The car bumped over a hump-backed bridge and the road narrowed. It was amazing how many inexplicably sharp bends there were when the landscape was so flat and straight. I must concentrate, I told myself.

But my mind darted back, all the same, to some of the sad souls I met when I was researching the Voices books. Tragically bereaved parents who found their way to Doris' door. People so stricken with grief, they didn't know how to go on living. People who could find no solace anywhere – religion, family, counselling, medication – nothing worked for them. They wrestled with pain so acute it was almost physical. Acquaintances would cross the road to avoid having to speak to them. And, frankly, as unkind as it sounds, you could see why.

Yet, Doris, having lost a child herself, couldn't turn them away if she could possibly fit them in.

'I promise you, the sun *will* shine again,' she'd assure them, settling them down with a cup of tea. 'It will. I've been there, luvvie, and I know, it does get better.' And then she'd call up her Voices and an hour or two later, they'd emerge from her flat, smiling for the first time, possibly in years.

Often, I'd speak to them in the months that followed. They nearly always said the same thing. Doris had turned their lives around. As a result of her words, they'd got their lives back and they could move forward. The sun *was* beginning to shine again for them, just as Doris promised.

Even if you were sceptical about the voices, how could you call that ruthless? Or even, wrong?

Still, there was no point in getting irritated. The roads were almost empty and I was nearly there. The tawny fields and gaunt trees of the open countryside were now dotted with weather-beaten cottages and soon the car moved into a large, cheerfully sprawling village.

Near the centre, I found Lyn's address and pulled up in front of a neat, brick-built bungalow.

Set back from the road, behind a long plot crammed with flowers, the bungalow looked out onto a tangle of September purples, reds and golds, all scrambling over each other in flamboyant cottage garden style. As I watched, the front door suddenly flew open, there was the sound of enthusiastic barking from inside, followed by much shushing, scuffling and banging of internal doors, and then Lyn appeared.

'Are you ok with dogs?' she asked.

I assured her I was.

'Well Cathy's shut them in the kitchen,' she said. 'But just in case!'

Lyn's hair was silvery now and she sometimes suffered from pain in her hip, but she was still straight and strong like the ice-skater she once was, before she got involved in the psychic world. She led me inside to the accompaniment of more yelping, excited canine cries, and possibly the thud of a furry body hurling itself against a closed door (in vain). The door remained resolutely shut.

Lyn bustled into the sitting room but behind her, as I reached the threshold, I actually stopped stock-still in amazement. There, on the opposite wall, was a large, oval, raised-relief picture of a pair of praying hands. The fingers long, slim and slightly knobbly were unmistakably spiritual. I hadn't remembered the piece but I recognised it instantly. The years fell away. I realised I'd seen that artwork every time I visited Doris' home. It had caught my eye the very first time I walked in to interview her for my supernatural series. Those hands had moved with Doris from one flat to another, and then to her house, and were always prominently displayed.

And now here they were, continuing their never-ending prayer on Lyn's wall.

'Well, I can see one of your successful bids already!' I said to Lyn. 'Doris loved that picture.'

Lyn smiled. 'I know.'

She knew, she explained because she was quite sure Doris had been guiding her since before the auction was even planned. Over a hearty salad, created by the irrepressible Cathy (now followed by two bouncing dogs, joyously released), Lyn told me the curious story.

As a small girl, she'd seen and made friends with other children, she said – children who seemed to be invisible to everyone else. At the time, though, Lyn didn't think of them as ghosts, or spirits. Possibly influenced by the new Dr Who TV series everyone was talking about, she assumed they were time travellers, exploring the past, from the future. So she drifted through her childish world seeing auras around people and sometimes coloured lights, but supposing this was the normal way of things.

Then, one morning, her life changed.

She was taken to an ice rink for the first time. She stared out in wonder at the pristine ice pad, stretching away into the distance, shimmering and perfectly white, with little wisps of mist rising off the surface like cold breath. She tasted the sharp, pure air, intoxicating as champagne, and she was utterly entranced. From that moment on Lyn was a skater, and eventually, when she grew up, a skating coach.

For many years, Lyn was too involved in the down to earth, competitive world of sport to give much thought to her odd childhood experiences. It was only when her father died that her attention began to shift.

'I was devastated,' said Lyn. 'So much so that, in the end, a friend – one of my athletes – who was also a spiritualist said I ought to come with her to Croydon Spiritualist Church. I wasn't sure about this idea at all, but she said she thought it would help me.'

Lyn was reluctant but eventually she agreed. At the church, much to her surprise, she found she liked the elderly medium who stood up at the front giving the congregation messages from departed loved ones. Strangely, she also noticed she seemed to be able to see many of the people the medium said she was talking to. Intrigued, she went back to the church the next time the medium was appearing. On this occasion, Lyn received messages too.

'She said she'd got my father there,' said Lyn, 'and he was saying 'Remember Flanagan and Allen? Me and My Shadow? Well I'll be your shadow now.' My father loved Flanagan and Allen and we used to sing that song together. I couldn't hear or see my father, unfortunately, but it's exactly what he would have said. There's no way the medium could have known the significance of that song for me.'

Lyn was so impressed that she wanted to know how it was done. She subsequently joined a developing circle – as medium training sessions are called – at her local church in Lewisham.

During a group meditation one evening, she had a strange vision. As if watching a film playing on the inside of her closed eyelids, she saw herself standing outside an impressive building that looked rather like a museum or grand Victorian library. A woman came up to her. This woman was tall with light, shoulder-length hair, and she said she was going to be Lyn's Co-operator in spirit. She didn't want to be called a guide, she said, but she was going to stick with Lyn from now on, through thick and thin.

Next, Lyn was whisked inside the building where she saw classrooms filled with students learning lessons. Then, she was outside again, and the woman pointed to a queue of people that had formed.

'There are some people here who've been waiting to see you,' she said, and as Lyn walked towards them she realised they were her relatives – her grandparents and other family members who'd passed away years before. She felt a great wave of love as they greeted her – so much so that she felt sad when the scene finally faded away.

From then on, Lyn explained, her Co-operator in spirit often came to chat to her. She wasn't shy about giving instructions either – even though at this point she hadn't revealed her name. One evening, she told Lyn she wanted her to give a message to Ron, the man in charge of the music at Lewisham Spiritualist Church.

'I was nervous but she kept insisting,' said Lyn, 'so in the end – before the service – I took a deep breath, went up to Ron who was standing near the kitchen door, and said, 'Could I give you a message please? 'Yes, of course, you can,' he replied, 'I like a message!' So I started to tell him what I'd been told to say. 'I've been asked to give you this woman's love and say how she loved the colour blue and there's a special rose bush outside her house. This rose bush is important. There's something around it or under it.'

There followed more personal information about Ron and his wife Vi and, by the time Lyn finished, Ron had gone white.

'I want you to tell Vi what you've just told me,' Ron said and he led Lyn over to where Vi was sitting at the door getting ready to greet the congregation.

'I was terrified, thinking I was going to be told off!' Lyn recalled. 'Ron took me to where Vi was sitting and said, 'Go on, tell her.'

'Well, Vi looked funny as she listened and then she asked, 'Who told you this? What did she look like?'

'She's tall with what looks like blonde hair, shoulder-length,' I said. 'Very tall and straight-backed wearing a long blue frock, and a lovely face and smile.'

'Yes, that's her,' Vi said. 'Did she give you her name?'

'Well, when I asked, she said it was Rose, and when I said that's a funny name for a guide she replied: 'A rose by any other name.'

'Vi said: 'We called her Duchess! But her name is Doris. Doris Stokes.'

Lyn was shocked. 'But she's famous and written books.' Not that Lyn had ever read any of the Voices series, but she was worried Ron and Vi would assume she'd picked up the information she'd given them from Doris' autobiography.

Vi shook her head. 'You couldn't have known what you've told us from her books. It wasn't in her books.'

She went on to explain that she and Ron had been old friends of Doris, John, and Terry.

'John was a healer here at the church too,' Vi went on. 'And Doris always told us that when she went over (died) she'd come back – but only through someone as different from herself as possible. She'd come through to a really tough woman who was not in our way of life. That's what she said. So here you are.'

It was a strange story. Yet, oddly enough, I recalled years ago Terry frequently referring to Doris as 'the Duchess', rather than 'Mum' for some reason. It puzzled me at the time. I never heard anyone else using that nickname. I think I assumed it must be something to do with Terry being adopted. Maybe he felt 'Mum' wasn't quite appropriate as she wasn't his biological parent.

Ron and Vi didn't explain the nickname either. Perhaps they'd simply heard Terry using it and copied him. At any rate, Doris obviously didn't object.

'Did they tell you why the rose bush behind the house was mentioned?' I asked.

'No,' said Lyn.

'Well I could be wrong,' I said, 'but she loved her Blue Moon rose bush. They planted it in the back garden and it was very special to her.'

What's more, not long before my visit to Lyn and Cathy, I'd been trying to research what happened to the Stokes' house after it was sold. Unexpectedly, I came across a little item that mentioned Doris Stokes' ashes had been scattered beneath her favourite rose bush in the garden of the property.

'So, maybe, that's why the rose was mentioned to you,' I said. 'Doris' ashes were underneath.'

Lyn was amazed. A quarter of a century on, she'd finally found out the significance of her message.

By now, convinced she was being guided by Doris, Lyn was very interested to read in Psychic News about the forthcoming auction of the Stokes' family mementoes.

'Then Doris told me she'd like me to attend. There were some items she wanted me to have, she said,' explained Lyn. 'I didn't know what she had in mind, but she just told me to go along and she'd tell me when to bid. It was a good thing she did because the room was crowded and I was stuck at the back behind some tall men and couldn't see a thing. I just raised my paddle when Doris told me to, and I ended up with an assortment of things. I didn't even know what I'd bought!'

As well as the picture of the praying hands on the wall, Lyn showed me a number of pretty crystal glasses she kept in a cabinet, some little ornaments, and a cut-glass rose bowl filled with red silk rosebuds. I didn't recognise the small pieces but the rose bowl looked familiar. At one point, I was sure it stood on the table, filled with identical roses, beneath Doris' wall of spirit children.

'The funny thing was,' said Lyn, 'as I was leaving the auction, a man came up to me to help me put my things in the back of the car. He'd bought some pieces too. He said he'd known Doris and he was sorry. He didn't explain. He just said that he was sorry.'

The man also told Lyn his name, and when she mentioned it to me I was astonished. I'd never met the man but his name was well-known to me, though I hadn't thought of it for years. Doris frequently mentioned him at one time because he caused her a lot of unhappiness. As she became well-known, this man would keep popping up in the media, criticising her, accusing her of being a fraud, and generally saying things that upset her. John and Terry loathed him.

He was entitled to his opinion, of course. He was clearly a lifelong sceptic and there was no way Doris would ever change his mind.

So given his opposition to her work, what on earth had prompted him to waste valuable time attending an auction of Doris' personal knick-knacks? Even more unlikely, why would he want to bid for some? I couldn't imagine. And, of course, Lyn – not knowing the history – hadn't thought to ask. A mystery.

But Lyn hadn't quite finished with the story of the auction items. When she got home and unpacked the box to see what she'd bought, she lifted out a couple of items and a small rectangle of white paper fluttered to the floor. She picked it up and turned it over. It was Doris Stokes' membership card for the Spiritualist National Union – now handed on to her.

'Quite a while after that,' said Lyn, 'I got up one morning and Doris told me I was to go to Stansted Hall and take Laurie O'Leary – her old manager – a silk rose from the rose bowl. Stansted Hall was quite a drive away and I couldn't think why Laurie would be there. He lived in London. It seemed like a crazy thing to do. It would have made more sense to go to his office. But she was so insistent that in the end I went.'

When she arrived at the country mansion, Lyn went up to the reception desk to ask if a Laurie O'Leary happened to be visiting. She fully expected the answer to be 'no' but, to her surprise, she was told he was there and they'd call him for her.

A few minutes later, a mystified Laurie O'Leary came down the sweeping staircase. He'd never seen Lyn before and had no idea who she was, or what she could want, but he was always polite and ready to listen. They moved to the easy chairs in the hall and sat down.

'This may sound mad,' said Lyn feeling a bit foolish, 'but Doris Stokes told me you'd be here...'

At the mention of Doris' name, Laurie probably gave an inward sigh. Since she'd passed away, he'd been inundated with requests from mediums who assured him Doris had been in touch and wanted her old manager to promote them now. Not one of them had convinced him. The last thing he needed was yet another hopeful thinking he could make them famous.

'...and...' Lyn continued, trying not to be discouraged by his unenthusiastic expression, 'she wanted me to give you this.' She opened her bag, took out the silk rose, and handed it to him.

For once, Laurie was speechless. He looked at the rose and tears filled his eyes. Apparently, before her operation, they'd agreed that if anything went wrong, Doris would send a message back to him from beyond. A message only Laurie would understand. And when it came, he would know it. Yet, so far, there'd been nothing.

But now... he turned the rose in his fingers and he cried.

It may have been he recognised the rose as belonging to Doris – he would have seen it often enough in the rose-bowl. Or it may have been that his mother's name was Rose. And Doris once told him, correctly, that he was so upset when he lost his mother that he kept her photograph hidden away in a drawer because he couldn't bear to see it.

Doris had told him his mother's name and said Rose wanted her picture brought out of the darkness and put on display on his desk. What's more, he was to put a flower in front of it for her. Which, of course, Laurie did from then on. And, though I don't know for a fact, I wouldn't mind betting the flower he put there most often was a rose.

So, for whatever reason, Laurie seemed to take that red silk rose as the message he was waiting for. As far as he was concerned, Doris had kept her promise. She'd reached out from beyond the grave and sent him the private message only he would understand.

And that, I thought, was probably the end of the story. But as it turned out, it wasn't, quite.

The next day, I emailed Lyn to thank her for a lovely afternoon and to say how much I enjoyed seeing Doris' things. And for some reason, I mentioned the big brown Shire horse which had been the only item I remembered in advance of my visit to the Fens. I wonder who ended up buying that, I wrote.

'Oh, the Shire horse!' Lyn replied. 'I forgot all about that. It was in the kitchen – that's where we keep it. Doris got me to bid for that too.'

Maybe she wanted to keep it out of my reach, in case I dropped it again!

So that was everything. Surely there were no more Doris references to come? I thought.

Wrong again.

A few months later, a friend invited me to one of those psychic fairs that seem to be springing up everywhere. It was in a small village hall on a minor road leading to nowhere in particular, and I didn't think many people would turn up. Yet, when we walked inside, the barn-style room was packed. There were stalls selling crystals and glowing salt lamps. There were hand-made greetings cards and tables of jewellery, there were books and feathery dream-catchers, and all manner of mystical odds and ends, as well as live Reiki healers and psychics of various kinds.

It was warm and colourful and everyone seemed to be enjoying themselves. At the far end of the hall, I could see a refreshment area where a couple of young women were frantically cutting sandwiches and dispensing generous chunks of cake. It looked appealing. A cup of coffee would go down well I decided, so I squeezed through the crowd and joined the queue. A moment later, an elegant woman approached. She'd been drawn to talk to me she explained later, but at the time I just thought we were chatting as we waited for our drinks. After a while, the conversation somehow turned to Doris Stokes.

'Her books changed my life,' said the woman. Her name was Lesley James she told me and she was a medium – though, like many others, she'd never intended to take up such a career. She came from a conventional Christian family – in fact her aunt was a missionary – and young Lesley was involved with her local, very traditional church.

Yet, when she was tragically and unexpectedly widowed, and found herself left with two small children to bring up alone, she found the grief hard to bear despite her faith.

'In the end someone gave me this book to read,' said Lesley. 'It was called Voices in My Ear. I don't think I'd even heard of Doris Stokes at that point and I didn't normally have much time for reading, but once I started the book I couldn't put it down. When it came to bedtime, I didn't want to stop.

'Unlike a lot of people, I don't like reading in bed. Can't seem to get comfortable somehow. So I went upstairs, got into my nightclothes, and took the book out onto the landing. I sat there on the floor, back against the wall, feet stretched out towards the banisters, reading away.

'After a while, I heard footsteps walking down the landing towards me. I thought it was one of the children on the way to the bathroom. I was so engrossed, I didn't even look up from the page – I just moved my legs so they could get past. But no one stepped over me and the feet stopped.'

Slightly impatient at the interruption, Lesley looked up to see what the child wanted, and her mouth must have dropped open.

'It wasn't one of the children,' she said. 'It was my father standing there. My father who had died years before. He didn't look like a ghost. He was as solid and real as he'd always been in life. I could see his boots, right next to me, pressing into the carpet, I could see the pile on his corduroy trousers and the rough texture of his tweed jacket. I could even smell the familiar scent of welding from the works where he was employed that always clung to his clothes.

'He looked down at me and nodded approvingly towards the book. 'I see you've found your path at last,' he said and he smiled.

And then somehow, before the shocked Lesley could even think of something to reply, he wasn't there anymore. He'd just gone.

'And that was what got me started on learning to be a medium,' said Lesley.

It was an extraordinary story and an extraordinary chance meeting. But then, by now, I'd heard so many extraordinary stories from so many extraordinary people.

So what to make of it all? So many voices over so many years, all describing things that science says is impossible.

Yet, to me, all of these people seemed sincere. Perhaps I'm credulous, perhaps I'm naïve – it's entirely possible, of course, and can't be discounted – but they didn't strike me as dishonest. They didn't strike me as liars or con artists. They genuinely appeared to believe the events they described, and they all gave the impression of being mentally competent in every way.

After a while, it struck me that though their experiences were varied in so many ways, it was almost as if they were talking about different facets of the same mysterious force. As if, without realising it, they were all talking about the same thing. And I get the feeling the conversation isn't over yet, because there really are voices everywhere.

SUCCESS IN THE YEAR OF THE RAT

2020

DARK RIVER

LINDA DEARSLEY

From Linda Dearsley, author of *Voices Everywhere* comes the third book in her Chinese Zodiac series – *Success In The Year of The Rat*.

January 25th 2020 sees the Chinese Year of the Rat begin. So what will the next 12 months bring to you?

Does the Rat present your astrological animal with opportunities or challenges? Whether your year animal gets on easily with the Rat, or has to work a little harder at the relationship, you can make 2020 a wonderful year to remember with this book.

Karina Collins is an acclaimed Tarot reader who has helped people, from all walks of life, to better understand their lives' journeys. Now, she is on a mission to help you take control of your life – through the power of Tarot – to better explore and understand *your* purpose and destiny.

In this unique full-colour book, Karina provides explanations and insights into the full 78-card Tarot deck, how to phrase questions most effectively, real-world sample readings, why seemingly scary cards represent opportunities for growth and triumph, and more.

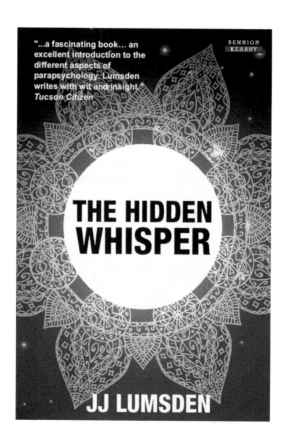

"...a fascinating book... an excellent introduction to the different aspects of parapsychology. Lumsden writes with wit and insight."
Tucson Citizen

BENNION KEARNY

THE HIDDEN WHISPER

JJ LUMSDEN

The Hidden Whisper is the acclaimed paranormal thriller, written by real-life parapsychologist Dr. JJ Lumsden, which offers a rare opportunity to enter the intriguing world of parapsychology – the study of the paranormal.

The narrative – exploring a poltergeist outbreak – is combined with explanations and references that cover Extra Sensory Perception, Psychokinesis, Haunts, Poltergeists, Out of Body Experiences, and more.

"This book works on many levels, an excellent introduction to the concepts current in the field of parapsychology... at best you may learn something new, and at worst you'll have read a witty and well-written paranormal detective story" parascience.

www.BennionKearny.com/paranormal

Milton Keynes UK
Ingram Content Group UK Ltd.
UKHW020818041123
431893UK00019B/845